Butterflies of India

Om Books International

To my wife Raka and son Shaurya with love

Reprinted in 2017 by

Om Books International

Corporate & Editorial Office
A-12, Sector 64, Noida 201 301
Uttar Pradesh, India
Phone: +91 120 477 4100
Email: editorial@ombooks.com
Website: www.ombooksinternational.com

Sales Office:
107, Darya Ganj,
New Delhi 110 002, India
Phone: +91 11 4000 9000
Fax: +91 11 2327 8091
Email: sales@ombooks.com
Website: www.ombooks.com

Design: Alpana Khare

ISBN: 978-93-80069-60-9

10 9 8 7 6 5 4 3 2

Printed in India

CONTENTS

INTRODUCTION

Butterflies are an abundant and diverse group of animals and a conspicuous part of virtually all the world's terrestrial ecosystems. They appeal to people in a unique way, and popular imagination often separates butterflies from insects, as if the former are an entirely distinct group of animals. The study and watching of butterflies perhaps ranks second only to ornithology as a pastime for naturalists. Unlike most other insects, including moths – their closest relatives – butterflies are accepted readily in cultures and celebrated in aesthetics. They are an important flagship group for advocacy of invertebrates, forming a bridge between the publicly acceptable world of conserving mammals and birds, and the widespread antagonism toward the mass of less conspicuous animals that dominate our natural world.

Butterflies belong to the order 'Lepidoptera' (scaly winged insects). These include moths (Heterocera) and butterflies (Rhopalocera), of which 17,000–20,000 taxa are butterflies. There is no precise estimate when butterflies evolved. The oldest fossil dates back to 48 million years. Various theories put the beginning of butterflies between 50 million and 170 million years, but they certainly evolved not later than the late Jurassic period. As there is no precise estimate, the period of their evolution is often termed the 'awkward age'.

IMPORTANCE OF BUTTERFLIES

Butterflies are important components of biodiversity, and are ecologically important due to the role they play in the food chain of a forest ecosystem. Their eggs, larvae (caterpillars), and adults (butterflies) form the food of a number of other arthropods, birds and reptiles. Most butterflies are pollinators of flowering plants. They have a symbiotic relationship with plant diversity as they are dependant upon a variety of plants for larval food. Butterflies are good biological indicators of environmental variation and quality. Being diurnal and conspicuously attractive, they are easily noticed flying around in the sunshine. Compared to other invertebrates, they are also an easily identifiable group being widely studied and with most species described in detail. They have short lifespans, are widespread, and occur in all types of habitats. They have been determined to be sensitive to, and directly affected by any alteration in their habitat and its climate. Butterflies are prime candidates in the tropics as well as in temperate regions for their use as indicators of conservation value, as they interact with a broad spectrum of ecological niches and microhabitats. Butterflies are being used as indicators of environmental variation, as some species have precise and restricted environmental requirements that reflect a particular suite of ecological conditions or indicate broader effects of environmental changes. A marked change in their distribution and abundance may be an early warning of the need for concern on a local or broader geographic scale.

Butterflies also hold great aesthetic value for humankind. Their shapes, colours, and patterns have always fascinated humans and are celebrated in art. The commercial value of butterflies has been realised in many countries located along the tropics. In Australia and USA, some species, e.g., the Monarch, are reared in large numbers on demand and released during special occasions like weddings, forming part of an industry. Butterfly farming, ranching, and breeding for butterfly mementos are part of the local livelihood in Papua New Guinea. Ecotourism in butterfly parks, gardens, conservatories, and trails is now practised in many countries in the tropical and temperate regions.

DISTRIBUTION OF BUTTERFLIES IN INDIA

About 1502 species have been described in India, which include nearly 100 endemics. India lies at the junction of the 'Palaearctic' and 'Indo-Australian' zoogeographic regions of the world, often referred to as the 'Oriental' region, if we exclude Australia. Important butterfly subregions in India are the following:

Trans-Himalaya: This region includes the cold desert areas with barren rocky snow-covered mountains, and the Himalayan dry temperate and alpine forests lying in the rain-shadow area. It extends from the Ladakh region of Jammu and Kashmir (J&K) to Lahaul and Spiti districts in Himachal Pradesh (HP) and the inner ranges of Garhwal in Uttarakhand above 3500 m. The fauna here is mainly Palaearctic. Butterflies are abundant from July to August.

Western Himalayas: This region includes the tropical moist deciduous, subtropical, moist temperate, subalpine, and alpine forests extending from J&K to HP and Uttarakhand, between 500 m and 4000 m. It is partly 'Palaearctic' and partly 'Indo-Australian'. Butterfly diversity peaks during the pre-monsoon (May–June) and again during the post-monsoon (September–October) seasons.

Eastern Himalayas: This is a region of humid, tropical wet evergreen and semi-evergreen, subtropical broad-leaved, pine and montane wet temperate forests extending from Sikkim to Arunachal Pradesh, including parts of northern Bengal. It represents the transition zone between Indian, Indo-Malayan, and Indo-Chinese subdivisions.

Northeast India: This includes the plains and non-Himalayan hill ranges with humid, tropical wet evergreen, semi-evergreen forests lying in Assam, Nagaland, Manipur, Mizoram, Meghalaya, Tripura, southeast Arunachal Pradesh, and parts of West Bengal. It is the junction of Central Asian and Chinese subdivisions of the Palaeartic region with the peninsular Indian and Malayan subdivisions of the Indo-Australian

Tawny Mime

region. Butterflies are more common from February to March and September to October.

Peninsular India: This region consists of the tropical dry and moist deciduous and thorn forests lying south of the Himalayas, east of the River Indus, and west of the River Brahmaputra. It shows affinities with the Malayan subregion and forms the major part of the Indian mainland.

Western Ghats: This region of dense evergreen and semi-evergreen, dry and moist deciduous forests, from the River Tapti in Gujarat up to Kanyakumari in Tamil Nadu, running parallel to the west coast of India is home to a number of endemics. Butterfly diversity is high from September to October in this region.

Andaman and Nicobar Islands: This region of mainly tropical wet and semi-evergreen, moist deciduous, littoral and swamp forests shows affinity with the Indo-Chinese and Malayan subregions.

HABITS OF BUTTERFLIES

Flight time: Most butterflies are diurnal, preferring bright sunshine to fly around in. Some species of the subfamily Satyriinae, e.g., Common Evening Brown *(Melanitis leda)*, and some skippers, e.g., Orange Awlet, *(Burara jaina)*, are crepuscular and active at dusk and dawn. Butterflies become inactive during windy or rainy weather, when they prefer to settle down on the undersurface of leaves of trees and bushes, or on twigs or crevices in rocks.

Seasonal variation: Many species show seasonal variations during the year. Thus, two different forms are produced having dissimilar markings, colours or shapes. This feature is mostly seen in the families Nymphalidae and Pieridae. In the Common Evening Brown, *Melanitis leda*; Peacock Pansy, *Junonia almana*; most of the Bush Browns, *Mycalesis* spp.; and Rings, *Ypthima* spp., the wet season form (wsf) bears a number of eyespots (ocelli) on the underside besides the streaking, and is also dark on the upperside. While in the dry season form (dsf), the wings are more angular, and eyespots are completely absent or reduced to minute dots, and the plain and unstreaked underside gives a leafy appearance. In the Himalayas, where spring and autumn broods occur, butterflies exhibit these two distinct forms. Such variations are a result of varying environmental factors and help the species in better camouflaging itself.

Dimorphism and Polymorphism: When male and female are dissimilar in appearance, they are called dimorphic, e.g., Great Eggfly, *Hypolimnas bolina*, and Danaid Eggfly, *Hypolimnas misippus*. Species in which the female occurs in more than one form are called polymorphic, e.g., Common Mormon, *Papilio polytes*—forms *cyrus*, *romulus* and *stichus*, and Pale Clouded Yellow *Colias erate*—forms *pallida* and *glicia*.

Camouflage Mimicry: Most butterflies are brightly coloured on the upperside of their wings. When they close their wings, the underside is visible and is usually dull, with its shape, colour and pattern suited for camouflage, e.g., the Orange Oakleaf, *Kallima inachus*, resembles a dead, dry leaf. In many species of Lycaenidae, the lowermost part of the hindwing, the tornal area, is brightly coloured (tornal lobe) and resembles the eye, while the tail on the wing-tip resembles the antennae. When both the hindwings are slowly moved up and down parallel to each other, they resemble the head of the butterfly. If the butterfly is attacked, only that portion of the wing is lost and the butterfly escapes, leaving a torn, inverted V-shaped gap on the hindwing.

Protective Mimicry: Many species of butterflies have poisonous or toxic chemicals that they accumulate from their larval food plants. These butterflies are usually brightly coloured (orange, red, yellow, black) so that predators know they have to avoid them. Examples are the Common Rose, *Atrophaneura aristolochiae*, and the Common Windmill, *Atrophaneura polyeuctes*. Some butterflies mimic these toxic species in appearance through their wing patterns, colours and shapes, though they do not feed on poisonous plants like *Aristolochia* and are palatable. However, predators usually avoid them in confusion. This is called 'Batesian Mimicry', and is advantageous when the 'model' is abundant and the 'mimic' is rare. In the Great Eggfly, *Hypolimnas bolina* (mimic), the female resembles the Common Crow, *Euploea core*, while in the Danaid Eggfly, *Hypolimnas misippus* (mimic), the female resembles the Plain Tiger, *Danaus chrysippus*. When two or more closely related species of unpalatable butterflies resemble each other, it is known as 'Mullerian Mimicry'. In this case, both the 'model' and 'mimic' have equal advantages but have different degrees of palatability and both need not be abundant, e.g., the pairs of Common Windmill *Atrophaneura polyeuctes*, and Great Windmill, *Atrophaneura dasarada*, and Dark Blue Tiger, *Tirumala septentrionis*, and Blue Tiger, *Tirumala limniace*.

Patrolling and Hilltopping: Males of certain species, such as the Indian Tortoiseshell *Aglais cashmiriensis,* and the Common Nawab, *Polyura athamas*, exhibit territorial behaviour and remain associated with certain patches of assorted food plants. These males take up perches on prominent positions such as treetops, from where they make sorties after any flying object. If a suitable female is encountered, they start

Painted Lady

courting. Intruding males are chased away and the territory is defended by patrolling. Males of certain species, e.g., Kaiser-i-Hind, *Teinopalpus imperialis*, in the hills establish themselves on a prominent spot on the summit or ridge, from where they patrol the area in search of receptive females and wander into the forest below only for nectar.

Basking: Butterflies are cold-blooded and cannot regulate their body temperature, as they cannot produce metabolic heat. They depend on the ambient temperature to do so. Thus, they remain inactive at night, coming out in the morning to bask in the sunshine. They do so also in the evening before sunset. Basking may be done dorsally, by wings spread wide open so as to maximise the surface area of absorption and by orienting the wings towards the sun. This can be seen in the Yellow Pansy, *Junonia hierta*. Basking may also take place from the lateral surface of the wings (underside) when they are clapped and held perpendicular to the sunrays, as in the Common Satyr, *Aulocera swaha*, and the family Lycaenidae. In white-winged butterflies, e.g., the Large Cabbage White, *Pieris brassicae*, wings are held at an angle (10° to 60°) in a V-shape so that they reflect sunrays directly to the thorax. The black area at the base of the wings absorbs the heat more effectively and the heat is transferred to the muscles.

Gully-bottoming: Butterflies of several species congregate in large numbers in shady *nullahs* and riverbeds during the hottest time of the day to cool themselves and avoid desiccation. This also helps in searching for mates, e.g., Large Oakblue, *Arhopala amantes*, and Tailed Punch, *Dodona eugenes*.

Floating: This is a very rare phenomenon that has been observed in the Yellow Pansy, *Junonia hierta*, in the lower western Himalayas. This species has adopted strange tactics to cool itself during the hottest time of the day. The butterfly slowly glides over the surface of shallow, non-turbulent, slow running water in forest streams under shade. At times, it falls on the surface of the water and floats for a few metres along with the current before flying away. This is repeated three to four times an hour during the hottest time of the day in the spring. The smooth metallic scales on the wings prevent it from drowning. The butterfly may do this with its dorsal or ventral side coming in contact with the water. Some Swallowtails such as the Jays, *Graphium* spp., have also been observed flying over the surface of free-flowing water in forested areas and momentarily touching the water surface while still in flight.

Sap-sucking: Many species of Nymphalids are attracted to the sap or gum present on a tree's stem that oozes out due to injury. Many species may congregate together at such spots. For example, the Grand Duchess, *Euthalia patala*; the Western Courtier, *Sephisa dichroa*; the Red Admiral, *Vanessa indica*; the Dusky Labyrinth, *Neope yama*; and the Common Forester, *Lethe insana*; feed together on sap exuding from the ban oak, *Quercus leucotrichophora*, trees in moist temperate forests of the western Himalayas.

Mud-puddling: Males of many species assemble on spots of ground contaminated with animal urine or excreta, or even the sweat of humans. These butterflies absorb from these sites essential elements such as sodium that have been lost during copulation in the form of sperms. Often, very large congregations of one or more species of butterflies congregate on these patches, but only males take part in the mud-puddling. The excess water that is absorbed is thrown out of the abdomen in the form of droplets.

Some nymphalids, such as the Common Jester, *(Symbrenthia hippoclus)* exude water in the form of droplets from the abdomen to moisten the dry ground surface on which the minerals are present. The moistened minerals can then be sucked.

Migration: As many as 60 species in India are migratory, and of these 33 are from the Himalayas. Two-thirds of these show only local migration. The most frequent of them are the Emigrants, *Catopsila pomona*; the Common Albatross, *Appias albina*; the Common Crow, *Euploea core*; the Blue Tiger, *Tirumala limniace*; the Striped Tiger, *Danaus genutia*; the Lime Butterfly, *Papilio demoleus*; the Great Eggfly, *Hypolimnas bolina*; the Painted Lady, *Vanessa cardui*; and the Peablue, *Lampides boeticus*. In the Himalayas, many species show seasonal migration along the altitudinal gradient to escape the harsh climatic conditions during winter, as they descend to the warm low-lying valleys in the foothills and adjoining plains during winter (September–December) and return to the higher reaches in the North to breed during late spring (March–May). Examples are the Pale Clouded Yellow, *Colias erate*; the Dark Clouded Yellow, *Colias fieldii*; the Bath White, *Pontia daplidice*; the Large Cabbage White, *Pieris brassicae*; the Indian Cabbage White, *Pieris canidia*; the Hill Jezebell, *Delias belladona*; the Common Emigrant, *Catopsila pomona*; the Club Beak, *Libythea lepita*; the Painted Lady, *Vanessa cynthia cardui*; the Orange Oakleaf, *Kallima inachus*; the Peablue, *Lampides boeticus;* and the Common Yellow Swallowtail, *Papilio machaon*. In South India, hundreds of milkweed butterflies such as the Dark Blue Tiger, *Tirumula septentrionis*; the Striped Tiger, *Danaus genutia*; the Common Indian Crow, *Euploea core;* and the Double-Branded Crow, *Euploea sylvester* migrate from the adjoining plains of southern India to the evergreen forests in the hills of the Western Ghats from November to February and go back to the plains from March to May every year.

WING MORPHOLOGY

FOREWING

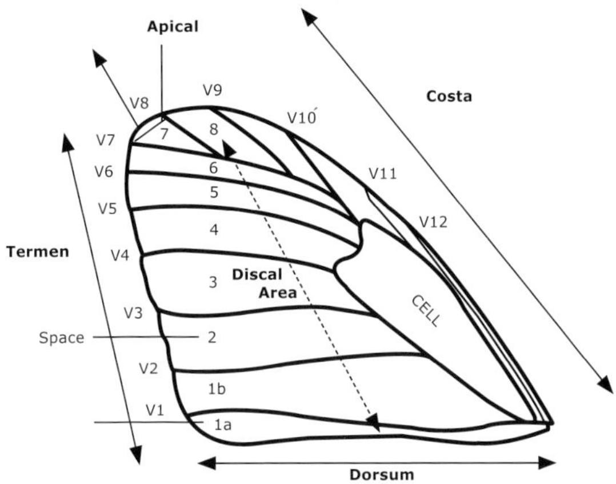

HINDWING

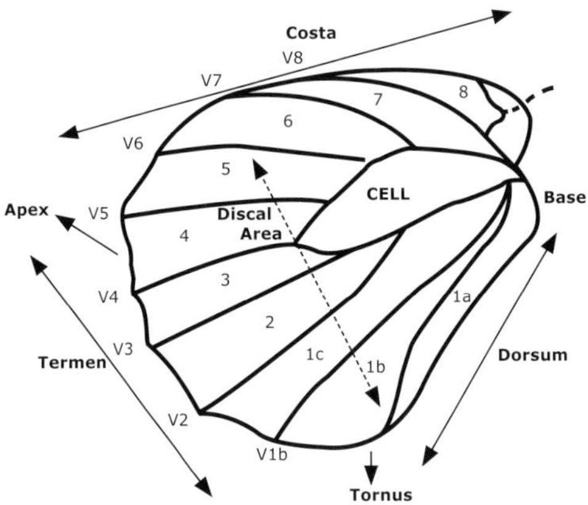

CLASSIFICATION OF BUTTERFLIES

Order: Lepidoptera (Butterflies and Moths): Scaly winged insects.

Suborder: Rhopalocera (Butterflies; 1502 species in India): Clubbed antennae.

Superfamily: Papilionoidea

Family:

1. Papilionidae (Swallowtails and Apollos; 107 species): Large butterflies with all legs fully developed. Hindwing usually tailed with concave inner margin and only one anal vein. Forewing vein in 3a free towards margin.

Subfamilies: Parnassinae (Apollos) and Papilioninae (Swallowtails).

2. Pieridae (Whites and Yellows; 109 species): All legs functional. Distinct bifid pretarsal claws. Hindwing with convex inner margin and two anal veins.

Pieridae family

Subfamilies: Pierinae (Whites); Coliadinae (Yellows).

3. Nymphalidae (Brush-footed butterflies; 522 species): Front legs useless for walking, brush-like in male, without claws. Antennal club usually very clear.

Subfamilies: Amathusiinae (Faun, Jungle Queens and Kings, Glories, Duffers, Caliphs); Satyriinae (Palmflies, Browns, Foresters, Labyrinths, Goldenforks, Walls, Rings, Argus, Satyrs) Calinaginae (Freak); Charaxinae (Rajahs & Nawabs); Apaturinae (Emperors, Princes, Courtiers, Courtesans); Nymphalinae (Castors, Yeomans, Silverstripes, Fritillaries, Pansies, Admirals, Tortoiseshells, Jesters, Eggflies, Oakleafs, Maps, Sailors, Sergeants, Commodores, Commanders, Barons, Dukes and Duchesses); Heliconiinae (Lacewings); Acraeinae (Costers); Danainae (Milkweed butterflies: Tigers and Crows); Libytheinae (Beaks).

4. Lycaenidae (Blues; 443 species): All legs functional, although males may have claws missing from front legs. Antennae bases adjacent to eyes, and often indented. Mostly rather small. Often metallic.

Subfamilies: Poritiinae (Gems); Lyphyrinae (Moth butterfly); Miletinae (Brownie, Darkie, Apefly); Curetinae (Sunbeams); Theclinae (Hairstreaks, Oakblues, Plushblues, Onyx, Silverlines, Royals, Tits, Sparks, Flashes); Lycaeninae (Coppers and Sapphires); Polyommatinae (Lineblues, Ceruleans, Pierrots, Hedge Blues, Jewels); Riodininae (Punches and Judies).

Superfamily: Hesperioidea

Family:

1. Hesperiidae (Skippers; 321 species): Antennae widely separated at base and gradually thickening to form club, which is often hooked at tip. Forewing with no stalked peripheral veins.

Subfamilies: Coeliadinae (Awls, Awlets, Awlkings); Pyrginae (Flats); Hesperiinae (Hoppers, Aces, Bobs, Demons, Darts, Swifts).

I. PAPILIONIDAE

COMMON MORMON • VERY COMMON

Papilio polytes (Linnaeus) 85–100 mm

Seen round the year throughout India, from plains up to 2000 m, in light-wooded country in hills. Fond of visiting flowers and dung, and can be seen mud-puddling in damp patches. Males usually perch together in a common roost in the evening and bask in sunshine in the morning. Male entirely black, with pale spots in middle of upper-hindwing, series of pale spots on margins of upper-forewing and red marginal crescents on underside of hindwing. Female occurs in three forms: *cyrus*, which resembles male but has prominent red marginal crescents on underside of hindwing; *romulus*, which mimics Crimson Rose but has bands on forewing that are not well formed and lacks black body; and *stichius*, which also mimics Common Rose but lacks red markings on body. Larval food plants: *Aegle marmelos, Citrus* spp., *Glycosmis arborea, Murraya koenigii, Zanthoxylum* spp.

♂

♀ **_Form cyrus_**

♀ **_Form romulus_**

♀ **_Form stichius_**

BLUE MORMON • NOT RARE

***Papilio polymnestor* (Cramer)** 120–150 mm

♂

Common in evergreen jungles of peninsular India and in Jharkhand, Bihar, West Bengal, and Sikkim. Found at heights between 670 m and 2000 m. Flight rapid and dodging. Frequently visits flowers like Lantana along forest paths and water. More common just after rains. Tailless butterfly with pale blue markings. Underside of hindwings has 2 rows of black dots on pale blue discal band, which narrows towards apex, where it is intersected with black ridges. Female has red spot at base of upper-forewing. Larval food plants: *Atalantia* spp., *Citrus* spp., *Glycosmis arborea, Paramigyna monophylla.*

BROWN GORGON • RARE

Meandrusa sciron **(Leech)** 105–115 mm

♀ UP

♂ UP

Flies across the Himalayas from Uttarakhand to Arunachal Pradesh. On the wing from April to October. Prefers well-wooded mountains (moist temperate broad-leaved forest) between 1400 m and 2500 m (western Himalayas). Usually encountered in damp patches near forest streams and flying high in canopy during sunshine. Females come down for egg-laying on the saplings of *Persea duthiei* (Lauraceae) (Kedarnath Sanctuary, western Himalayas). Female more common than male, and can be distinguished by the presence of broad white discal band, which is dark brown in male.

GOLDEN BIRDWING • NOT RARE

Troides aeacus **(C.R. Felder)** 120–190 mm

♂

♀

Flies across the Himalayas from Uttarakhand to Arunachal Pradesh. Common in summer (May–June) in forested valleys up to 1800 m, where it sails under canopy and

settles on flowers *(Aesculus indica, Bauhinia vahlii)*. Upper-hindwing bright yellow, with cone-shaped black marginal markings and black veins. Female has a series of black spots inside yellow area and broad grey vein stripes. Two red spots just below the base of underside of wings near thorax.

COMMON WINDMILL • LOCALLY COMMON

Atrophaneura polyeuctes (Doubleday) 110–140 mm

Locally common. Distributed across the Himalayas from J&K to Arunachal Pradesh. Recorded from April to September between 1200 m and 2500 m (western Himalayas). Flies in long circles, often high over trees, where usually a few individuals assemble on flowers (*Clematis* spp., *Aesculus indica* and *Citrus* spp.). This large red-bodied Black Swallowtail has twin red spots on tail. Hindwing long and narrow, with large oblong white discal patch between v4 and v5 and small white patch below this, between v3 and v4. Underside of hindwing has 3 red spots along margins. Larval food plant: *Aristolochia* spp.

ROSE WINDMILL • RARE

Atrophaneura latreillei (Donovan) 110–130 mm

Occurs across the Himalayas from HP to Arunachal Pradesh. Flies from April to July between 1500 m and 2000 m (western Himalayas). Flight leisurely. Prefers forested areas, forest edges and flowering trees. Large red-bodied Swallowtail with red-tipped tail. Upper-hindwing of male has white elongate and conical discal spots in spaces 2, 3 and 4. Spot in space 3 larger than others. Upper-hindwing has submarginal crimson crescents in spaces 2–5. Females a bit paler, with larger white and crimson markings on both sides of hindwing. Larval food plant: *Nepenthes* spp.

GREAT WINDMILL • NOT RARE

Atrophaneura dasarada (Moore) 100–140 mm

Flies across the Himalayas from J&K to Arunachal Pradesh. Woodland species that prefers forest openings between 1200 m and 2700 m. Flight period from April to July. Fond of visiting flowers. Has a series of white and red spots on upper-hindwing with female having complete discal band of white spots on upper-hindwing from spaces 1–4. Tail red-tipped. Larval food plant: *Aristolochia* spp.

COMMON ROSE • COMMON

Atrophaneura aristolochiae (Fabricius) 80–110 mm

UP

UN

Occurs throughout India in open deciduous forests from plains up to 2400 m. On the wing from July to October in northern India. Flies low over undergrowth with help of only forewings. Red-bodied Swallowtail with elongated forewings that have pale grey stripes in distal part of cell and between veins. Hindwing has 5 elongated spots, out of which 4 are white, while lower one near body is pink and has on margin series of up to 7 red crescents. Larval food plant: *Aristolochia* spp.

CRIMSON ROSE • LOCALLY COMMON

Atrophaneura hector **(Linnaeus)** 90–110 mm

♂

Occurs in southern India, Orissa, Jharkhand, West Bengal, and the Andamans. Flies throughout the year. Prefers shady areas in forest habitats to visit flowers. Roosting congregations often seen. Black Swallowtail with bright crimson spots on hindwing. Prominent white discal and apical bands on forewing. Mimics Common Mormon form *romulus*. Body crimson. Female dull with larger crimson markings. Larval food plant: *Aristolochia* spp.

SPANGLE • COMMON

Papilio protenor **(Cramer)** 100–130 mm

Found from J&K to Arunachal Pradesh in the Himalayas in forested tracts up to 2500 m. Flight period from April to July. Prefers nectar, feeding on flowers in forest openings and gardens. Flies rapidly over undergrowth and often observed mud-puddling. Large tailless black butterfly. Male has black-centred red spots on upper-hindwing, while female has additional black-centred red spot in space 2. Blue scaling visible on upper-hindwing. Male has broad red dorsal stripe on underside of hindwing. Larval food plants: *Murraya koenigii, Zanthoxylum alatum.*

UP

RED HELEN • LOCALLY ABUNDANT

Papilio helenus (Linnaeus) 110–130 mm

Occurs in South India (Western Ghats) and across the Himalayas from Uttarakhand to Arunachal Pradesh. Prefers evergreen forests, where it flies from April to November from the terai up to 2100 m. More common in South India. Flight slow, but dashes away when disturbed. Visits flowers and wet ground. Basks in sunshine in the morning and after rains. Forewings folded back while resting, concealing white markings. Large black butterfly with series of three creamy white spots in spaces 5 to 7. Underside of wings has series of red crescents forming row on margins. Larval food plants: *Evodia* spp., *Glycosmis arborea, Toddalia asiatica, Zanthoxylum* spp.

LIME BUTTERFLY • COMMON

Papilio demoleus (Linnaeus) 80–100 mm

Distributed throughout India. Prefers open areas, gardens, and hedgerows up to 2000 m in the hills. Flies throughout the year. Often observed mud-puddling in large numbers along with other butterflies. Tailless black-spotted yellow butterfly. In older individuals, yellow markings turn to almost deep orange. Upperforewing has tornal red spot and apical black and blue spot. Larval food plants: *Aegle marmelos, Citrus medica, Glycosmis arborea, Limonia acidissima, Murraya koenigii.*

COMMON YELLOW SWALLOWTAIL • UNCOMMON

Papilio machaon (Linnaeus) 75–90 mm

Distributed across the Himalayas from J&K to Arunachal Pradesh. Flies throughout the year. Comes down to lower valleys in the Himalayan foothills (650 m, Dehradun) in winter, but can be seen during summer in high mountainous alpine vegetation till highest tree line (4800 m). Flies fast and over long distances. Prefers forest openings with good undergrowth and flowering shrubs in temperate forests. Tailed black and yellow butterfly, with upper-forewing cell and veins outlined in black. Cell has black bar in middle and another bar at end. Margins black, with a series of regular small yellow spots near termen. Blue-topped red spot at tornus. Larval food plants: *Daucus carota, Heracleum* spp. *Selenium* spp.

TAILED JAY • COMMON

Graphium agamemnon (Linnaeus) 85–100 mm

UP

UN

Found across India, including the Andaman and Nicobar Islands, from plains up to heights of 1800 m. Common in forested tracts that receive good rainfall. Flies from March to November. Restless butterfly, flying from flower to flower and feeding on nectar while hovering. Blackish butterfly with bright green spots and markings and short stout tail. Two red spots, each edged with a black crescent, near base. Tornal spot on underside of hindwing. Larval food plants: *Annona squamata, Artabotrys hexapetalus, Miliusa tomentosa, Polyalthia longifolia, Cinnamomum* spp., *Michelia champaca, M. doltsopa.*

COMMON BLUEBOTTLE • COMMON

Graphium sarpedon (Linnaeus) 80–90 mm

UP

Found across the Himalayas in forested areas from J&K to Arunachal Pradesh up to 2700 m. Flies from March to October. Restless and a fast flier. Visits flowers, bird droppings, carcasses and wet ground. Black butterfly with greenish-blue central band running on the inside of both wings. Band broken into spots in forewing apex; narrows at both ends. Underside of hindwings has a few red spots in black portion. Hindwings extended in form of short tails. Larval food plants: *Miliusa tomentosa, Polyalthia longifolia, Cinnamomum camphora, Litsea chinensis, Persea odoratissima, P. macrantha.*

GLASSY BLUEBOTTLE • LOCALLY COMMON

***Graphium cloanthus* (Westwood)** 82–95 mm

Found throughout the Himalayas from J&K to Arunachal Pradesh, from foothills up to 2800 m. More common in open country between 1200 m and 1800 m in the western Himalayas. Visits flowers (Horse Chestnut and *Buddleia*) and wet sand, where males congregate. On the wing from April to October. Long-tailed black and blue butterfly with black border and pale blue central band that enters cell of upper-forewing and is wider than in Common Bluebottle. Light blue colour semi-transparent, hence the name Glassy. Veins of forewing black and broad. Four pale green, semi-transparent spots on black border at termen of hindwing. Basal red spots with black centre on underside of hindwing. Larval food plants: *Miliusa velutina, Persea duthiei, P. odoratissima, Michelia* spp.

UP

UN

COMMON MIME • FAIRLY COMMON

Form *dissimilis*

Form *clytia*

***Chilasa clytia* (Linnaeus)** 90–100 mm

Occurs across the Himalayas from HP to Arunachal Pradesh, as well as in southern, central, and northeastern India. Seen mud-puddling and nectar-feeding on flowers in well-wooded areas up to 2000 m. More abundant in dry weather. Tailless butterfly occurring in two forms: *clytia*, which is dark and mimics Common Crow; and *dissimilis*, which mimics Blue Tiger in pattern but lacks blue colouration. Prominent yellow marginal cells on underside of hindwings present in both forms. Larval food plants: *Alseodaphne semecarpifolia, Cinnamomum zeylanicum, Litsea* spp.

TAWNY MIME • LOCALLY COMMON

***Chilasa agestor* (Gray)** 80–120 mm

Found across the Himalayas from J&K to Arunachal Pradesh. Occurs between heights of 1200 m and 2500 m. Flies from March to May. Flight is sailing on top of bushes, and without flapping of wings. Tailless butterfly resembling Chestnut Tiger. Upper-forewings grey, with veins on outer margins, similar to Chestnut Tiger, but without the glassy markings. Upper-forewings have black bars across cell near apex and submarginal crescents instead of spots. Upper-hindwing has submarginal lunules instead of spots. Larval food plants: *Cinnamomum* spp., *Persea odoratissima.*

COMMON PEACOCK • COMMON

Papilio polyctor (Boisduva)l 90–130 mm

Occurs in the Himalayas from J&K to Arunachal Pradesh in mixed moist deciduous to moist temperate forests from 600 m to 2200 m. Flies from March to October. Fast-flying butterfly that prefers open, sunny, and rocky areas. Comes to flowers and water. Males often seen mud-puddling. Tailed butterfly with dusted, pale metallic green scales and blue iridescent patch on hindwing that does not enter cell, and whose inner edge is straight but diffused. Up to 4 red crescents present along margin on the upperside of hindwing. Larval food plants: *Zanthoxylum armatum, Z. acanthopodium, Clausena* and *Citrus* spp.

UP

UN

PARIS PEACOCK • UNCOMMON

Papilio paris (Linnaeus) 90–140 mm

Found across the Himalayas from Uttarakhand to Arunachal Pradesh and Central and Northeast India. Confined to moist evergreen forests from 1500 m to 2000 m in the Himalayas. Flies from March to November. Usually seen along forest streams, on flowers, mud-puddling, and hill-topping. Quite similar to Common Peacock, but blue iridescent patch on hindwing large and enters cell, and its inner edge curved and sharply defined. Tornal spot on upper-hindwing. Larval food plants: *Zanthoxylum ovalifolium, Z. oxyphyllum, Toddalia asiatica, Evodia* spp., *Citrus* spp.

MALABAR BANDED PEACOCK • RARE. LOCALLY COMMON OTHERWISE

Papilio buddha (Westwood) 90–100 mm

Endemic to Western Ghats from Goa to Kerala, where it occurs in evergreen and semi-evergreen forests. Flight period from May to October. Males engage in hilltopping. Females uncommon. Black-bodied Swallowtail with broad rich greenish iridescent central band entering cell on upperside of both wings. Tail black. Larval food plant: *Zanthoxylum rhetsa.*

SPOT SWORDTAIL • LOCALLY COMMON

***Graphium nomius* (Esper)** 75–90 mm

Found in peninsular India as well as in Gujarat, Madhya Pradesh, Chhattisgarh, UP, Uttarakhand and Arunachal Pradesh. Prefers moist deciduous forests up to 1000 m. Common from March to June (single brooded in northern India), when seen mud-puddling on moist sand, generally in open forest and along streams. Black-and-white butterfly with broad, white-spotted outer margins on upperside of wings. Cell region has broad bars including at the end, where basal one reaches v1 and another reaches dorsum. Underside of hindwing has a row of prominent central red spots and long sword-like tail. Larval food plants: *Miliusa tomentosum, M. velutina, Polyalthia longifolia.*

UP

UN

SIX-BAR SWORDTAIL • EXTREMELY LOCAL

Graphium eurous (Leech) 60–70 mm

UP

UN

Occurs in the Himalayas from J&K to Arunachal Pradesh and in the hills of Northeast India between 1000 m and 2800 m. Prefers forest openings that have water. Males glide high, close to tree canopy, while females fly close to ground over undergrowth, visiting flowering shrubs to feed on nectar. Abundant during spring (March to May; single brooded). Whitish semi-transparent butterfly, with 6 dark bars on cell and long sword-like tail. Underside of hindwing has marginal bands and complete row of central pale spots, of which tornal ones are yellow. Larval food plants: *Persea duthiei, P. odoratissima, Michelia doltsopa.*

KAISER-I-HIND • RARE AND VERY LOCAL

Teinopalpus imperialis (Hope) 90–120 mm

Found in well-wooded mountainous regions of eastern Himalayas (from Sikkim to Arunachal Pradesh) and in the hills in Northeast India between 1800 m and 3000 m. On the wing from April to July. Flies from morning till noon in sunshine. Does not visit flowers or wet sand and prefers to suck moisture from leaves. Males found on top of hills, and are territorial. Females also fly in cloudy weather. Males have prominent yellow discal area between spaces 4 and 8. In females, this area greyish, with only base of space 2 being yellow. Female also larger than male. The common name Kaiser-i-Hind literally means *Emperor of India.* Much sought after species by butterfly collectors for its beauty and rarity. Now globally threatened (classified as Lower Risk/ Near-Threatened species in IUCN's 2008 Red List of Threatened Animals) and protected under Indian wildlife laws. Larval food plant: *Magnolia campbelli.*

♂ UP

♀

♀ UN

COMMON BLUE APOLLO • LOCALLY COMMON

Parnassius hardwickii (Gray) 50–65 mm

Distributed across the Himalayas from J&K to Sikkim, between 2500 m and 3300 m. On the wing from March to October in western Himalayas. Prefers forest edges and alpine meadows, where it flies close to ground. Settles on grass and rocks along trails. White apollo dusted with black scaling on upper-forewing. Upper-forewing has 3 black bars on cell. Beyond third bar towards apex is series of black spots arranged in curved line along discal area. Termen broadly black. Red-centred spot at base of space 1. Upper-hindwing has 2 red-centred spots, one near base of space 5 and other in middle of space 7. Series of 5 black-ringed, white-centred blue spots arranged in arc on upperside of hindwing. These blue spots prominent only during wet season and reduced to smaller and lighter black spots in dry spring and summer months. Larval food plant: *Saxifraga* spp.

II. PIERIDAE

PSYCHE • COMMON

***Leptosia nina* (Fabricius)** 20–35 mm

UP

Found across India, including the Andaman and Nicobar Islands. Forest-loving species that prefers to fly slowly close to ground in undergrowth. Prefers to settle near ground on dry twigs. While resting, forewings folded into and below hindwings. More common in plains and the Himalayan foothills up to 1900 m. Small white butterfly with rounded wing. Upper-forewing has black apex and large black discal spot. Underside of hindwings has numerous fine greenish strigae (lines) that camouflage it in its surroundings. Larval food plants: *Cleome viscosa, Capparis* spp., *Crataeva adansonii.*

GREAT BLACKVEIN • LOCALLY COMMON

Aporia agathon (Gray) 40–90 mm

Found across the Himalayas from J&K to Arunachal Pradesh. Prefers mixed oak forests (western Himalayas) between 1200 m and 3000 m. Flies from March to July. Single brooded. Nectar-feeding takes place on flowers of *Aesculus indica* and *Berberis* spp. Mating occurs in oak forests during dry summer (May) in shade of undergrowth. White butterfly with all veins broadly blackened. Base of wings has yellow spot. Found in three races. Race *phryxe* found in western Himalayas (Kashmir to Uttarakhand) has broadly blackened veins with black expanding and meeting at termen to form narrow black border. Race *caphusa* distributed from Mussoorie to Kumaon has veins more broadly blackened than *phryxe*. Has very broad terminal and discal bands and the upper-forewing cell is dusted with black. Race *agathon* found from Garhwal to Arunachal Pradesh has entire basal half of upper-forewing dusted with black. Black markings broadest in *agathon*. Larval food plants: *Berberis lycium, B. nepalensis.*

♂ Race phryxe UP

♂ Race phryxe UN

♀ Race phryxe UP

Race caphusa

HIMALAYAN BLACKVEIN • COMMON

***Aporia leucodice* (Eversmann)** 40–70 mm

♀

Distributed across the western Himalayas from Kashmir to Uttarakhand. Prefers open areas in temperate forests at heights of 1200 m to 2800 m. Flies from May to June. Favourite haunt is Horse Chestnut *(Aesculus indica)* on which it flies slowly from flower to flower. White butterfly with thin black veins and no black dusting on upper-forewing. Larval food plant: *Berberis lycium.*

GREEN-VEINED WHITE • LOCALLY COMMON

Pieris napi (Linnaeus) 50–60 mm

Distributed across the Himalayas from J&K to Arunachal Pradesh. Prefers forest areas close to streams. More common in dry season at heights between 2000 m and 3500 m. White butterfly with blackened veins. Apex of forewing black, and black spot present on costal margin of hindwing. In female the markings are darker, with 2 black spots on upper-forewing. Underside yellowish, with greenish veins. Larval food plants: *Sisymbrium* spp., *Reseda* spp., cabbage.

UP ♂

UP ♀

UN

INDIAN CABBAGE WHITE • VERY COMMON

***Pieris canidia indica* (Evans)** 45–60 mm

Found across India but mainly in the hills up to heights of around 3600 m. Flies slowly and close to ground. Migrates from the plains to hills during late spring (April–May) in the Himalayas and back to plains in autumn (October–November). Visits flowers and wet ground. Black-and-white butterfly with male having 1 black spot and female 2 black spots on forewing. Inner margin of black apex toothed on upper-forewing. Underside marked with yellow on base of costa. Larval food plants: *Nasturtium* spp., *Rorippa dubia*, *Sisymbrium* spp., cabbage and related plants.

♀

♂

LARGE CABBAGE WHITE • VERY COMMON

Pieris brassicae **(Linnaeus)** 65–75 mm

Occurs across the Himalayas from J&K to Arunachal Pradesh up to 4000 m. Migrates from the hills to the plains in winter. Comes to flowers in open wooded and cultivated areas. Uphill migration takes place during summer (April in Northwest Himalayas). After summer migration, one generation is completed in foothills (on ornamentals such as *Nasturtium* spp.) and new generation undertakes ascent to higher hills. Upper-forewing black-tipped and plain white with no markings. Upper-hindwing completely white. Under-forewing has 2 black spots in female. Under-hindwing pale yellow with no markings. Larval food plant: Cabbage (Cruciferae).

♂

♀

♂

♀

BATH WHITE • COMMON

***Pontia daplidice* (Linnaeus)** 45–60 mm

Distributed in the western Himalayas from J&K to Uttarakhand, from the foothills 600 m to 2700 m. Migrates to foothills (Dehradun) in winter and back to higher reaches in spring (May). Prefers irrigated agricultural land at lower elevations and grassy patches in temperate spots. Under-hindwing has green patches. Female has a discal spot on the upper-forewing and rows of obscure terminal and marginal spots on the upper-hindwing. Larval food plants: *Lepidium virginicum, Sisymbrium altissimum.*

♂

♀

PIONEER • VERY COMMON

Belenois aurota (Fabricius) 40–55 mm

Prefers open dry regions across India up to 2800 m in the Himalayas. More common in the Shivaliks. Seen round the year but only seasonally in the Himalayas. Prefers wet sand and flowers. Forewing has a broadly-streaked white apex and a bar at the cell end. Hindwing has a white-spotted black border. Underside varies from white to yellow, and has black veins. Black-edged spots of earthen colour on the termen. In females, the black markings are thicker and broader. Larval food plants: *Capparis* spp., *Maerua oblongifolia*.

♂

♀

UN

COMMON GULL • VERY COMMON

***Cepora nerissa phryne* (Fabricius)** 40–65 mm

♂ DSF

♀ DSF

Found throughout India, including the Andaman and Nicobar Islands, up to 1200 m in the Himalayas and 2400 m in the hills of South India round the year. Prefers open dry areas, degraded forest and scrubland. Visits flowers and wet sand. Upperwings white with blackened veins. Upper-forewing has black terminal border with white spots. Under-hindwing pale or dark yellow, with veins heavily outlined in dark green. Black markings more extensive in males, especially on margins of cells. Forewing has additional black spot in 1b. Markings reduced in dry season. Larval food plants: *Capparis decidua, C. sepiaria, C. zeylanica.*

♀ WSF

♂ WSF

YELLOW ORANGE TIP • COMMON

***Ixias pyrene* (Linnaeus)** 50–70 mm

Distributed across India up to 2100 m in the Himalayas and 1800 m in the hills of South India. More common in the Shivaliks in the North. Prefers dry thorny scrub, mixed deciduous forest, and open areas. Seen round the year. Visits damp patches and flowers. In males, upper-forewing yellow, with orange band inside a black apical half. Upper-hindwing is yellow with black border. In females, upper-forewing more extensively white and orange patch in forewing reduced and faded, and bearing two black spots. Whitish form found in southern India and yellow form in northern India. Larval food plants: *Capparis decidua, C. divaricata, C. sepiaria, C. zeylanica.*

♂

♂

♀ yellow form

♀ white form

CRIMSON TIP • UNCOMMON

***Colotis danae* (Fabricius)** 40–50 mm

Distributed from peninsular India up to Madhya Pradesh and in Northwest India from Gujarat to Punjab. Prefers arid and semi-arid regions with grassland. Common during post-monsoon season (September–October) but can be seen flying throughout the year in South India. Flies very close to ground, where it feeds on nectar of small flowers. Small white butterfly with crimson apical patch on upper-forewing. Black spots present along termen of the upper-hindwing in male, while in female this spotting forms black band. Female has greyish dusting on base of upperside of both wings. Line of black spots runs from crimson area of upper-forewing to middle of upper-hindwing. Small black spot at end-cell of upper-forewing in both sexes. Larval food plants: *Cadaba fruiticosa, Capparis divaricata, C. sepiaria, Maerua oblongifolia.*

♂

♀

WHITE ORANGE TIP • COMMON

***Ixias marianne* (Cramer)** 50–55 mm

♂

Found throughout India up to 2000 m in hills, but more common in foothills. Flies rapidly and prefers open areas in mixed deciduous forest and scrub. Settles on wet ground and flowers on shrubs. White butterfly with black apical half in upper-forewing enclosing large orange patch. Terminal border of hindwing also black. In females, orange patch narrower and bearing 4 black spots. Wet season form more heavily marked on upperwings. Larval food plants: *Capparis* spp., *Maerua oblongifolia.*

REDSPOT JEZEBEL • NOT RARE

***Delias descombesi* (Boisduval)** 65–90 mm

Distributed in the eastern Himalayas from Sikkim to Arunachal Pradesh, from terai up to 1500 m. Flies throughout the year at lower altitudes. Prefers lowland forests and comes to flowering trees (*Moringa* spp.) in open areas of forests. Under-hindwing yellow, with red crescent patch along costa, and black border with pale yellow spots. Male white, with black apex and narrow black costa and termen on upper-forewing. Female has brownish black upper-forewing with white spot at end-cell, and pale marginal spots and veins. Its upper-hindwing is pale yellow with spotted border.

♂

COMMON JEZEBEL • VERY COMMON

***Delias eucharis* (Drury)** 66–83 mm

♀ UP

♂ UP

UN

Found throughout India except in arid regions. Fond of visiting flowers, flies slowly over trees and bushes. Colourful butterfly with yellow ground colour on under-hindwings intersected by black veins and red spots pointing outwards at outer margin. Under-forewing white with black veins. In females, upperwing white with tinge of yellow and pink. Markings on upper-wings heavier in females than in males. Larval food plants: *Viscum* spp., *Loranthus elasticus, L. scurrula, L. longiflorus.*

HILL JEZEBEL • COMMON

***Delias belladonna* (Fabricius)** 80–100 mm

Found across the Himalayas from HP to Arunachal Pradesh between 500 m and 3000 m. Common from summer to post-monsoon (April–October) season in the hills. Migrates down to the foothills and the Shivaliks during winter. Found close to streams on wet sand. Visits flowers (*Aesculus indica, Prunus* spp.). Flight slow. Black butterfly with a series of pale spots on upperwings. Upper-hindwing has dark yellow spot at base of costa, and yellow tornal patch and whitish dorsal area. Under-hindwing black with yellow cell spot, terminal and basal yellow spots, and discal spots varying from white to yellow. The race becomes darker as one goes East from western to eastern Himalayas. Larval food plants: *Dendrophthoe* spp., *Loranthus vistitus, L. longifolius.*

UP

UN

CHOCOLATE ALBATROSS • LOCALLY COMMON

Appias lyncida (Cramer) 55–70 mm

♂

Found from Uttarakhand to Arunachal Pradesh in regions below 1000 m, and in Orissa, Jharkhand, South India and Nicobar Islands. Prefers tropical moist deciduous and evergreen forests, where it can be seen flying fast close to wet ground along river banks and forest edges. Seen throughout the year in South India. Upper-forewing white with black spots inwardly toothed on termen. Hindwing has terminal spots. Upperwings bluish in colour. Underside bright yellow with chocolate border. In females, upper-forewing black with 4 white discal streaks, and upper-hindwing dark except for white discal area. Larval food plants: *Capparis cleghornii* and *Crataeva adansonii.*

MOTTLED EMIGRANT • COMMON

Catopsilia pyranthe (Linnaeus) 50–70 mm

Found across India up to 2700 m in the Himalayas. Common in urban gardens and open forest. Comes to flowers and wet ground. Migrates to higher reaches in the Himalayas during late spring from adjoining plains. White butterfly with black apical and marginal border on upper-forewing. Underside mottled with brown lines and red-ringed silver spot in centre of wings. In females, black markings broader and cell spot larger on the upper-forewing. Larval food plants: *Cassia fistula, C. auriculata, C. tora, Sesbania bispinosa.*

♂

COMMON WANDERER • COMMON

Pareronia valeria (Cramer) 65–80 mm

Distributed across India up to 1500 m in the Himalayas. Flies from April to November. Prefers forest openings, where it settles on flowers. Upperwing of male pale blue with black margin, prominent veins and marginal spots. Female whitish, less blue, and with black markings more prominent. Female of form *philomela* has yellowish colour at base of upper-hindwing. Larval food plants: *Capparis rheedii, C. zeylanica.*

♀
Form *philomela*

♂

♀

COMMON EMIGRANT • VERY COMMON

Catopsilia pomona (Fabricius) 55–80 mm

♂ *catilla*

Distributed across India up to 4000 m in Himalayas. Flies throughout the year at lower elevations. Found in all types of habitats, but prefers gardens, agricultural fields, scrub, and openings in the forest. Congregates during migration on wet ground. Colouration and markings vary considerably in this species, from yellow to translucent greenish white. Antennae may be black or red. Underside of wings may be unmarked or with red-ringed silver spots in centre. Female of form *catilla* has purple-brownish patches on the underside of wings. Larval food plants: *Bauhinia racemosa, Cassia fistula, C. siamea, C. tora, Butea monosperma.*

♂ UP

UP

♀ *catilla* UP

UP

COMMON BRIMSTONE • COMMON

***Gonepteryx rhamni nepalensis* (Doubleday)** 60–70 mm

Distributed across the Himalayas from J&K to Arunachal Pradesh between 1000 m and 2400 m. Flies from February to December. Comes down to foothills and valleys during extreme winter. Prefers open areas, grassland biomes, and flowering trees and bushes. Male yellow, while female translucent white. Both sexes have orange spot at end-cell on both wings. Outer margin and apex of hindwing both toothed. Larval food plants: *Vaccinium* spp., *Rhamnus dahuricus*.

♂

♀

SMALL GRASS YELLOW • COMMON

Eurema brigitta (Cramer) 30–40 mm

Distributed across India up to 3600 m in the Himalayas, being more common in the foothills. Flies from March to April and again from September to November. Prefers open degraded forests, where it flies around bushes. Yellow butterfly with outer margins of both wings black, black margins being broader in female. Two black spots at end-cell on underside of forewing. In wet season form, colours brighter. Larval food plant: *Cassia* spp.

♀ UP

♂ UP

UN

SPOTLESS GRASS YELLOW • COMMON

Eurema laeta (Boisduval) 30–45 mm

Found throughout India up to 800 m in the Himalayan foothills. Prefers forest openings and dry areas. Flies round the year. In dry season form, apex pointed and outer margins straight. Upperforewing has black apex. Underside pale in colour, with brown and pink scales and 2 straight lines running across hindwing. In wet season form, apex and termen wide and black, with inner edges rounded, while upperhindwing has narrow terminal border. Underside of forewing has small black spot in cell. Larval food plant: *Cassia* spp.

UP

UN

COMMON GRASS YELLOW • VERY COMMON

Eurema hecabe **(Linnaeus)** 35–50 mm

Seen across India up to at least 1000 m in the Himalayas. Flies round the year. Prefers to fly low among bushes, wet ground, and flowers. Male yellow, with apex and termen on upper-forewing and terminal border of upper-hindwing being broadly black. In female, black borders wider. Underside of forewing has two black spots in cell. Wet season form has brighter colour. Dry season form has narrower black markings on upperside and rusty markings on hindwing. Larval food plants: *Caesalpinia* spp., *Cassia* spp., *Acacia* spp., *Albizia* spp., *Sesbania bispinosa, Pithecolobium dulce.*

DSF UN

WSF UN

THREE-SPOT GRASS YELLOW • COMMON

***Eurema blanda* (Boisduval)** 40–45 mm

UN

Found across peninsular India and from Uttarakhand to Arunachal Pradesh in the Himalayan foothills, in regions up to 1000 m. Flies from March to May and again from September to November. Found in forested areas, mostly moist deciduous, and often seen flying over trees and bushes. Three black spots in cell on underside of forewings distinctive. Rusty markings present on underside of forewings in dry season forms. Other markings similar to *E. hecabe* on upper-forewing. Larval food plants: *Cassia* spp., *Delonix regia, Albizia* spp., *Pithecolobium dulce.*

PALE CLOUDED YELLOW • FAIRLY COMMON

***Colias erate* (Esper)** 45–55 mm

♂ *Form glicia* UP

♀ *Form glicia* UP

♀ *Form pallida* UP

Found in the western Himalayas and the foothills between 600 m and 3600 m. Flies from February to December. Migrates to lower altitudes in winter. Flies fast and close to ground. Visits flowers along streams and agricultural fields. Male pale lemon yellow, with black outer border on upper-forewing. No spots on black border in males; in females, uneven yellow spots. Distinctive black spot in disco-cellular region. Underside has two red-ringed silvery spots on cell in hindwing. In form *pallida*, female pale green with white spots on black border of upper-forewing. In form *glicia*, both sexes have upper-forewing spotted with ground colour.

DARK CLOUDED YELLOW • COMMON

Colias fieldii (Ménétriés) 40–65 mm

Distributed across the Himalayas from J&K to Arunachal Pradesh between 1000 m and 3660 m. Flies throughout the year. Migrates to lower valleys in winter. Prefers to feed on small flowers close to ground. While resting, wings closed. Upperside orange with black border. Border spotless in males but ringed with orange-yellow spots in females. Large black spot on end-cell of upper-forewing. Orange patch and black border faintly visible on the underside of forewing, which also has a white-centred black disco-cellular spot. Underside of hindwing greenish yellow, with two red-ringed pale spots. Larval food plants: *Indigofera* spp., *Medicago* spp., *Trifolium* spp.

♂

♀

III. LYCAENIDAE

COMMON GEM • UNCOMMON BUT LOCALLY ABUNDANT

***Poritia hewitsoni* (Moore)** 30–38 mm

♂ UP

Found across the Himalayas from Uttarakhand to Arunachal Pradesh from 300 m to 1000 m. Flight period from March to November in the western Himalayas. Usually encountered in moist deciduous forest openings and edges, basking on top of leaves of shrubs. Sexes dissimilar. Male upperwing brilliant blue, with broad black apex and costa with blue spots. Female brownish, with violet blue patches and yellow discal patch above blue area, merging with black apex. Underneath greyish brown, with numerous brownish bands and spots. Larval food plants: *Shorea robusta* and *Terminalia tomentosa* (Dehradun, western Himalayas).

♀ UP

♀ UN

INDIAN SUNBEAM • UNCOMMON

Curetis thetis (Drury) 40–48 mm

Occurs on Indian mainland common before and after the rainy season. Large Sunbeam with glossy white underwings and practically no black spotting or markings. Male has golden red upperwings, with narrow black borders in dry season. In wet season form border wider in males. Female has black border on white wings. Larval food plants: *Abrus precatorius,Derris scandens, Pongamina pinnata, Xylia dolabriformis.*

♂

♀

♀ **UP**

BRIGHT SUNBEAM • UNCOMMON

Curetis bulis (Westwood) 35–45 mm

Distributed across the Himalayas from HP to Arunachal Pradesh up to 2000 m from April to November. Males usually encountered in damp patches on ground or on leaves. Flight swift. Male bright orange. Upper-forewings have black apex and termen. Silvery white underneath, with black spots. Discal band under is straight, forewing pointing towards apex. Female black-and-white on upper-forewing. Hindwing termen sharply angled and concave.

♂ **UP**

ANGLED SUNBEAM • LOCALLY COMMON

***Curetis acuta* (Moore)** 35–42 mm

Found across South, Central, and Eastern parts of India, and the Himalayas from HP to Arunachal Pradesh up to 1300 m. Flies from March to November. Prefers damp patches. Settles on leaves and bird droppings on bushes in forest openings and tea gardens. Male territorial and more common than female. Upper-forewing of male has more extensive red area and black bar at end-cell more prominent than in Bright Sunbeam male. Only red discal patch visible in otherwise dark upper-hindwing. In female, white area on upper-hindwing more extensive than in Bright Sunbeam.

♂ UP

♀ UP

UN

WATER HAIRSTREAK • LOCALLY COMMON

***Euaspa milionia* (Hewitson)** 30–34 mm

UP

UN

Found across the western Himalayas from J&K to Uttarakhand. Seen in shady hillsides in oak forests between 1500 m and 2000 m near water, where it perches close to ground. Found from April to July. Chocolate-brown tailed butterfly, with broad white band running across wings from underneath. Series of conical brown-centred white spots on margins of wings and large black-centred orange spot on tornus of underside of hindwing. Male irridescent sky blue on upperside, with broad black apex, and white patch in discal area on forewing. Female dull blue with black apex on upper-forewing.

WHITE-SPOTTED HAIRSTREAK • LOCALLY COMMON

Euaspa ziha (Hewitson) 35–38 mm

Distributed across the western Himalayas from J&K to Uttarakhand. Found around its food plant, the ban oak *(Quercus leucotrichophora)* in moist temperate forests from 1500 m to 2200 m from May to July. Comes down on damp ground. Underneath, greyish white. Tailed butterfly with brown discal bar on under-forewing. Bar along margin has 3 prominent black spots in tornal region of under-forewing instead of 2 as in Walnut Blue. Under-hindwing has one to two orange-crowned black spots in tornal region. Upperside greyish blue. Upper-forewing apex and broad margin brownish, with 2 white spots, with one present beyond cell and the other between v3 and v4.

UP

UN

SILVER HAIRSTREAK • COMMON

***Neozephyrus syla* (Kollar)** 42–45 mm

♂ **UN**

♀ **UN**

Found across the Himalayas from J&K to Arunachal Pradesh from 1800 m to 2400 m. Common in oak forests from May to October. Prefers wet ground close to forest streams in dry season. Male shining metallic green, with bronze gloss and even-sized black border. Female iridescent blue, with broad black border, cell and apex pale silvery blue. Hindwing greyish black, with dusting of blue scales. Underneath silvery grey with brown submarginal and broader discal bars, outwardly bordered white.

♀ **UP**

♂ **UP**

♀ **UP**

♂ **UP**

UN

FAWN HAIRSTREAK • LOCALLY COMMON

***Neozephyrus birupa* (Moore)** 38–40 mm

♂ UN

Distributed across the western Himalayas from HP to Uttarakhand. Flies from April to October from 1500 m to 2100 m, but abundant during late spring (May, Mussoorie). Found close to water in dry weather, when both sexes can be seen on wet ground. Tailed butterfly with greyish light brown colour underneath wings. Bar at end-cell and discal band running from costa to vein 2 on under-hindwing. Black-centred orange spot and orange black-edged crescent marking on tonus of under-hindwing. On upperside, male metallic green, with 2 mm border on both wings. Female brown, with blue in discal area below cell. Has large white discal spot on upper-forewing. Larval food plant: *Rhododendron arboreum.*

♂ UP

♀ UP

LARGE OAKBLUE • LOCALLY COMMON

***Arhopala amantes* (Hewitson)** 45–57 mm

Seen across the Himalayas, from terai up to 1500 m, from HP to Arunachal Pradesh; West Bengal, Bihar, Jharkhand, peninsular India up to Gujarat and Madhya Pradesh. Prefers damp ground in tropical moist deciduous forests from March to October. Converges on shady *nullahs* in dry hot season. Male brilliant dark blue, with thin black border, while female paler with broad black border. Underside pale greyish brown with dark brown white-edged spots and bands of spots. Under-forewing has 3 spots in cell, of which spot at base is smallest. Larval food plants: *Terminalia alata, T. catappa, T. paniculata, Lagerstroemia microcarpa, L. flos reginae, Xylia xylocarpa.*

♂ **UP**

♀ **UP**

♀

♀ **UN**

INDIAN OAKBLUE • COMMON

Arhopala atrax (Hewitson) 34–40 mm

♀ UP

♂ UP

Seen across the foothills of the Himalayas from HP to Arunachal Pradesh up to 1800 m, West Bengal, Orissa, Chattisgarh, Jharkhand, Madhya Pradesh, all year round, being more common during pre-monsoon and post-monsoon periods. Prefers damp patches in tropical moist deciduous sal forests. Male dusky purple, with brownish borders at apex, while female purple-blue with broader border, toothed at end-cell. Blue may be absent on hindwing of female. Hindwing tailed. Underneath, pale greyish brown. Tornal green scales are present on hindwing. Larval food plant: *Shorea robusta.*

DUSKY BUSHBLUE • RARE

Arhopala paraganesa (de Nicéville) 32–37 mm

Seen across the Himalayas from Uttarakhand to Arunachal Pradesh from 900 m to 1800 m in moist temperate forests from March to September. Underside pale creamy white with chocolate brown markings. Upperside pale violet blue with broad black border broadening at apex. Spot present at end-cell. Larval food plant: *Quercus leucotrichophora.*

UP

LYCAENIDAE

DARK HIMALAYAN OAKBLUE • COMMON

***Arhopala rama* (Kollar)** 34–40 mm

Occurs across the Himalayas from J&K to Arunachal Pradesh and Northeast India. Prefers oak forest between 1200 m and 2800 m. Congregates in shady *nullahs* in dry season. Forewing apex pointed sharply concave below point. Underneath greyish brown with silky gloss. Hindwing with non-metallic green tornal scales. Markings obscure. Male purple with black borders which are broader on hindwing and extend a little way along dorsum on forewing. Female has wider border and purple only just beyond cell. Toothed end-cell on forewing. Underside forewing discal line continuous, not dislocated. Larval food plant: *Quercus leucotrichophora.*

♀ UP

♀ UN

♀ UP

UN

PALE HIMALAYAN OAKBLUE • COMMON

***Arhopala dodonea* (Moore)** 38–44 mm

Occurs in the western Himalayas from J&K to Uttarakhand from May to October. Prefers oak forest between 1200 m and 2800 m. Swarms in shady *nullahs* in dry season. Under-forewing discal line continuous, not dislocated. Forewing termen wavy. Below, pale gloss on silky, creamy brown wings. Above pale blue. Broad black border of 4 mm. Forewing and hindwing borders broad, veins blackish. Larval food plant: *Quercus leucotrichophora.*

UP

UN

SPANGLED PLUSHBLUE • NOT RARE

***Flos asoka* (de Nicéville)** 40–44 mm

Occurs across the Himalayas from Uttarakhand to Arunachal Pradesh and Northeast from foothills up to 700 m. Flies during pre-monsoon (June, western Himalayas). Prefers openings and wet ground along streams in moist deciduous forest. Metallic green scales underneath; lobe prominent. Dark basal band to dorsum. Borders narrower in male, tailed and lobed. Underneath, discal spots in spaces 6 and 7 more disconnected and irregular; inner edge of spot in space 6 not in line with inner edge of spot on end-cell. Forewing less pointed.

♂ UP

♀ UP

UN

UN

COMMON ACACIA BLUE • FAIRLY COMMON

***Surendra quercetorum* (Moore)** 30–40 mm

Found in South India, Jharkhand, Northeast India, and lower Himalayas from HP to Arunachal Pradesh up to 1200 m. Flies from March to November. Prefers deciduous hill forests. Perches on twigs or leaves of trees and bamboos. Flies briefly and comes back to same perch. Male dark brown, with middle of forewing disc purple-blue. Hindwing purple from above. Female dark brown with pale light brown on disc. Dark brown below, with very narrow dark markings, some of which are outwardly silver edged. Highly irregular disc line and marginal dots. Male with 1 and female with 2 tails. Larval food plants: *Acacia pinnata, A. caeisa.*

♂ UP

♀ UP

UN

SILVERSTREAK BLUE • UNCOMMON

Iraota timoleon **(Stoll)** 40–48 mm

Found all across India except in arid and semi-arid areas up to 2000 m in the Himalayas from HP to Arunachal Pradesh. Flies from April to November. Prefers to settle on foliage of shrubs and fig trees and other treetops. Flight swift. Male shining blue above, with broad black border on apex of both wings. Underside dark reddish brown with silver streak in cell of forewing and discal spots. Hindwing ochreous towards margin with broad irregular basal streak silver or reddish ground in colour and with zig-zag discal markings. Female above with a shining purple discal patch on brownish wings. Male has one tail, while female is double-tailed. Larval food plants: *Ficus glomerata, F. religiosa, F. virens.*

♂ **UP**

♀ **UP**

UN

REDSPOT • UNCOMMON LOCALLY

Zesius chrysomallus (Hübner) 38–44 mm

Occurs in peninsular India, Bengal, Bihar, Orissa, UP, and Uttarakhand (670 m, Dehradun). Prefers deciduous forests with shade, and gardens, where it perches high on bushes. Male more common; coppery-red from above with narrow, dark brown borders. Hindwings have 2 red-crowned tornal spots and 2 tails. Female pale powdery blue above, with broad, borders, and is three-tailed. Pale grey below with discal band of loosely-linked spots. Several cell and basal spots. Red crowned spot in 2.

♂ UP

♀ UP

YAMFLY • LOCALLY COMMON

Loxura atymnus (Stoll) 36–40 mm

Found across the Himalayas from Uttarakhand to Arunachal Pradesh up to 950 m, UP, Bihar, West Bengal, Northeast India, Jharkhand, and South India up to Maharastra. Flies from April to December. More common during monsoons in damp patches. Perches on shrub leaves near its larval food plants, *Dioscorea pentaphylla* and *Smilax* spp. Hindwings form a long white-tipped tail. Underneath ochreous with a few dark spots and faint outcurving band on both wings. Orange above with broad black apex and border.

UP

UN

COMMON ONYX • LOCALLY COMMON

Horaga onyx (Moore) 27–33 mm

Distributed across the Himalayas from HP to Arunachal Pradesh and Western Ghats. Prefers thick mixed forest tracts, and canopy of litchi and mango trees. Flies in the Himalayan foothills from 600 m to 2000 m from March to November. Dark yellowish brown butterfly from underneath, three-tailed and with variable broad white discal band on both wings. Underneath forewing, white discal band and dark line bordering it extend almost up to costa. Another irregular dark wavy line with metallic green border runs along margin of the hindwing above the two black spots on margins. Upperside of both sexes blue with apex, termen and costa black, and prominent white discal patch on upper-forewing. Larval food plant: *Coriaria nepalensis* (the Himalayas).

UP

UN

BROWN ONYX • UNCOMMON

***Horaga viola* (Moore)** 22–28 mm

Distributed across the Himalayas from HP to Arunachal Pradesh, Northeast India and the Western Ghats. Prefers mixed moist deciduous forest tracts and litchi orchards in the Himalayan foothills from 600 m to 1000 m. More common during post-monsoon period from October to November, and from January to February in the South. Small brown butterfly from above, with 3 tails and white discal patches on forewing. Underneath forewing, white discal band and dark line bordering it extends up to the costa. The white marking on the hindwing faint and reduced but bordered by dark line on innerside, which extends and bends up to dorsum. This line is bordered by a metallic green border, where it bends up to the dorsum. Another irregular dark wavy line with metallic green border runs along margin of hindwing above 2 black spots on margins. Larval food plant: *Coriaria nepalensis* (the Himalayas).

UP

UN

COMMON IMPERIAL • LOCALLY COMMON

Cheritra freja (Fabricius) 38–42 mm

UP

Found across the Himalayas from Uttarakhand to Arunachal Pradesh and the Western Ghats at lower elevations (below 800 m), from April to December. Prefers clearings in wet hill forests. Found on ground, undergrowth and rocks close to streams. Has 2 white tails, upper being straight and longer than the lower one on hindwing. Underside pale brown to white, with faint discal and marginal lines and narrow dark outer discal line. Black spots crowned with metallic blue or orange scales at tornus. Larval food plants: *Cinnamomum* spp. and *Xylia xylocarpa.*

DARK BLUE ROYAL • RARE

Pratapa icetas (Hewitson) 30–38 mm

UP

UN

Distributed across the Himalayas from HP to Arunachal Pradesh from 1500 m to 2500 m. Flies in dry season; pre-monsoon (March-May) and post-monsoon (September-October). Prefers moist temperate forests, where it comes to ground. Underside pale grey, with a continuous dark grey discal line from forewing costa to hindwing dorsum. White bars are present at end-cells. Upper-hindwing lobe orange with 2 orange-crowned black spots on hindwings. Male shining blue, with broad black apex, while female pale violet-blue, with some white area on upper-forewing. Upper-hindwing dark brown, dusted with blue scaling.

TUFTED WHITE ROYAL • UNCOMMON

Pratapa deva (Moore) 32–40 mm

Found across India except desert regions, and across the Himalayas from HP to Arunachal Pradesh up to 2000 m. Flies from April to November. Prefers forested hillsides. Double-tailed butterfly with creamy white underside. Outer discal line not continuous and bars at end-cell faded. Two orange-bordered black spots on hindwing. Male shining blue on the upperside, with wide black apex. Female greyish blue from above. Prominent veins visible on upper-hindwing. Larval food plants: *Dendrophthoe falcate, Loranthus scurrula, L. tomentosa, L. longifolius.*

♂ UP

♀ UP

UN

PLAINS BLUE ROYAL • NOT RARE

Tajuria jehana (Moore) 30–36 mm

Found across southern India up to Goa; the Himalayas from Uttarakhand to Sikkim up to 2000 m, and West Bengal. Flies from May to November in wooded areas with ephiphyte *Dendrophthoe* spp., its larval food plant. Double-tailed butterfly with white hairs along wing margins. Underneath, pale grey to white, outer discal line and bars at end-cell on forewing faint or absent. Underneath hindwings, discal line is broken at v3 and v4, tornal markings prominent. Male slaty blue above with broad black apex, while in female, the blue area more extensive. Area beyond cell whitish. 2 tornal black spots present on upper-hindwing.

♂ UP

♀ UP

UP

PEACOCK ROYAL • UNCOMMON

***Tajuria cippus* (Fabricius)** 30–45 mm

Found across India except in desert and semi-desert areas up to 2000 m. Prefers openings and flowering trees *(Syzygium operculatum, Tamarindus indica)* and wet ground in deciduous forests. In flight from May to October. Has 2 white-tipped tails. Black spots at tornus bordered by orange crown. Underneath pale grey with a series of interrupted thin black lines near outer margin of wings. Male brilliant metallic greenish sky blue, with broad black apex from upperside. Female slightly larger than male and pale greyish blue. Has several black spots along termen and a series of curved black lines along post-discal region. Larval food plants: *Loranthus* spp., *Dendrophthoe falcata*, *Helicanthus elastica*, *Helixanthera wallichiana.*

♂ UP

♂ UN

♀ UP

♀ UN

STRAIGHTLINE ROYAL • UNCOMMON

Tajuria diaeus (Hewitson) 33–36 mm

Distributed across the Himalayas from HP to Arunachal Pradesh and Northeast India. Flight period from June to November. Flies between 1500 m and 2500 m. Prefers oak forest. Brownish grey below, with prominent dark straight outer discal line continuous between termen and end-cell. Sky blue above; apical half of forewing black. Female is pale blue, with white spot beyond cell on forewing. Larval food plant: *Loranthus longifolius.*

CHOCOLATE ROYAL

Remelana jangala (Horsfield) 32–42 mm

Found across eastern Himalayas from Sikkim to Arunachal Pradesh; terai up to 1000 m from March to December. Common at lower elevations (200 m) in winter. Visits flowers (*Ageratum* spp.) and damp patches. Double-tailed butterfly with chocolate-coloured underside. Tornal spots on hindwings crowned with metallic green line and irrorated with white patches at three places. Upperside of male brownish black, with lustrous purple-blue; central patch from base to discal area. Female paler than male. Larval food plant: *Rhododendron* spp.

UN

BI-SPOT ROYAL • UNCOMMON

Daclana ctesia (Hewitson) 38–40 mm

♂ UP

♂ UN

Distributed across the Himalayas from Uttarakhand to Arunachal Pradesh and Northeast India between 1400 m and 2000 m. Flies from April to October. Common in forest openings and edges with streams and wet ground. Tailed butterfly, with silver grey ground colour below. Broad bar at end-cell, and discal band consisting of line of black spots. Male shining blue above, with large black spot on dorsum and also one in discal area on upper-forewing. Female purple-blue turning whitish towards apex. Black spots absent in female. Larval food plant: *Viscum* spp.

COMMON TIT • COMMON

Hypolycaena erylus (Godart) 32–36 mm

♂ UP

♀ UP

UN

Found in the eastern Himalayas from Sikkim to Arunachal Pradesh, from terai up to 1300 m, Northeast India and the Andamans. Flies from April to December. Common around damp patches. Two-tailed butterfly that is pale grey on the underside. Double bars present at end-cell. Discal line narrow and continuous on the forewing but broken on the hindwing. Prominent yellow-crowned tornal spot in space 2. Male is a dark shining purple on the upperside and has a dark area. Female is brown with a white discal band above tornus and a black tornal spot that is white-edged in space 2. Larval food plants: *Cinnamomum zeylanicum, Meyna pubescens, Vangueria spinosa.*

BLUE TIT • LOCALLY COMMON

Chliaria kina (Hewitson) 26–29 mm

Found across the Himalayas from Uttarakhand to Arunachal Pradesh between 1000 m and 2000 m. Flies from March to October. Prefers to settle on wet ground and undergrowth in forest edges. A double-tailed pale grey butterfly on the underside with black-edged grey markings. Male is pale blue with a black border; the inner area has violet spots. Female is dark brown from above with a white discal area. Veins of upper-hindwing dark. Tornal spot orange-crowned.

♂ UP

♂ UN

FLUFFY TIT • UNCOMMON

Zeltus amasa (Hewitson) 28–32 mm

Distributed across India from Sikkim to Arunachal Pradesh, northern part of West Bengal, Northeast India and part of the Western Ghats below Goa. Found from terai up to 1000 m. Flies from April to December. Male inhabits open areas, forest edges, gardens and wet ground. Has two long, fluffy tails. Underside pale ochreous-brown with dark markings. Double lines at end-cell. Discal line continuous with underneath forewing but broken below at veins 3, 4, and 6. A prominent black spot present at space 7. Tornal spot prominent. Upperside of male is pale blue with broad black apex. The female is dark brown.

♂ UP

♂ UN

ORCHID TIT • LOCALLY COMMON

Chliaria othona (Hewitson) 24–27 mm

Occurs across the Himalayas from Uttarakhand to Arunachal Pradesh up to 1500 m, Northeast India, West Bengal, Western Ghats, and the Andamans. Flies from February to December. Seen in damp patches inside moist deciduous and evergreen forests with epiphytic orchids. More common during June. Hindwing has two tails. White butterfly from underside with faint bars at end-cells and black-edged brown markings. Discal band broken at v4; with upper part of band broader than lower part, in both wings. Prominent small black spot in space 7 towards base. Tornal spot large and orange-crowned. Male pale blue above with broad black apex, and termen with deep purple blue spot. Female brown with lower part of discal area whitish. Larval food plants: Epiphytic orchids, e.g., *Rhynchostylis retusa.*

♂ UP

♂ UN

UN

GUAVA BLUE • COMMON

Deudorix isocrates (Fabricius) 34–50 mm

Distributed throughout India up to 2100 m, except in arid regions. Fond of flowers. Pale greyish brown underneath with dark markings. Discal band straight on under-forewing. Hindwing has 2 black tornal spots. Male dull brown on upperside, with purple scales. Upper-forewing of male has black costa and margin. Hindwing metallic purple, with slightly toothed termen that has a tornal lobe. Female is brownish and larger than male and with dull orange patches at end-cell of upper-forewing and black-centred orange tornal spot. Larval food plants: *Tamarindus indica, Strychnos nux vomica, Psidium guajava, Punica granatum, Gardenia latifolia.*

♂ UP

♀ UP

UN

LARGE GUAVA BLUE • UNCOMMON

Deudorix perse (Hewitson) 48–52 mm

Distributed across the Himalayas from HP to Arunachal Pradesh up to 1000 m, and South India up to Maharastra. Prefers forested areas; orchards, comes to flowers. Flies from March to November. Underneath light brown with discal band consisting of linked spots much darker than ground colour. Discal band bent on forewing midway. Spot at base of 7 on under-hindwing. Upperside of forewing of male shining blue, with wide brown termen, apex and costa. Cell black, with dark orange patch beyond cell. Upper-hindwings have wide brown costa and apex. Female paler with blue on upperwing and pale patch on upper-forewing. Larval food plant: *Catunaregam spinarum.*

♂ UP

♀ UP

♀ UN

UN

CORNELIAN • UNCOMMON

***Deudorix epijarbas* (Moore)** 34–44 mm

♂ **UN**

♂ **UP**

Found across India except in arid regions, up to 2000 m in the Himalayas. Occurs from April–December. Shape appears like triangle when wings are closed. Underneath dark brown with brown, white-edged discal bars. Hindwing lobe black and orange-crowned. Has single tail. In male, upperside tawny red. Outer margins of forewing have wide black border. Black-centred orange spot on tornal lobe of upper-hindwing. Female duller and paler than male, with more brown colour. Larval food plants: *Connarus wightii, Punica granatum, Aesculus indica, Litchi chinensis, Sapindus marginatus, S.trifoliatus.*

♂ **UP**

♂ **UN**

BROAD SPARK • RARE

***Sinthusa chandrana* (Moore)** 28–32 mm

♂ UP

♂ UN

Found across the Himalayas from HP to Arunachal Pradesh and Northeast India up to 1800 m. Flies from May to November in the western Himalayas. Prefers dense forest edges, openings, and gardens. Comes to flowers for nectar feeding. Male is deep shining purplish blue. Upperside of the hindwing also has black border on upper part. Upper-forewing dark with bronzy gloss. Female has dark brown upperside. Underside pale greyish brown with end-cell bar and discal bands. Discal band on forewing broken at v4. Very irregular and broken into 5 parts on hindwing, broad dark grey and white-edged. Hindwing has small lobe and tail.

COPPER FLASH • LOCALLY COMMON

***Rapala pheretima* (Hewitson)** 38–42 mm

♂ UN

♂ UP

Distributed across India from Sikkim to Arunachal Pradesh, Northeast India, West Bengal, Jharkhand and Orissa. Common from terai to 1500 m in the Himalayas, from March up to December. Prefers to feed on flowers (*Ageratum* spp.). Upperside dark copper-red, with broad black apex and termen black. Upper-hindwing coppery red. Female purplish with brownish border. Underneath yellowish brown with prominent dark brown markings, white on outer edge. End-cell bar prominent.

INDIAN RED FLASH • LOCALLY COMMON

Rapala iarbus (Fabricius) 33–41 mm

Found across India except in arid regions of Northwest and Northeast India up to 2000 m in the Himalayas. Found mainly in tropical moist deciduous forests in foothills, the Shivaliks and plains. Prefers to settle on undergrowth, dry leaves and wet ground in the forests. Upperside forewing bright orange, with purple gloss and dark brownish borders narrowing to tornus and blackened veins. Hindwing red, with black tornal lobe crowned red with metallic scales. Female coppery red, with broad dark borders and duller in colour than male. Underside slaty grey, having a thin discal line with 2 tornal spots one being orange-crowned. Larval food plants: *Ougeinia dalbergioides, Zizyphus rugosa.*

♂ UP

♂ UN

UN

SLATE FLASH • COMMON

Rapala manea (Hewitson) 30–33 mm

Found across India except in arid regions, and up to 2000 m in the Himalayas. Found throughout the year, but more common during pre-monsoon to post-monsoon seasons. Prefers flowers and wet ground. Settles on leaves of shrubs where it prefers to bask. Upperside of male slaty-blue with more brilliant colour in discal area of both wings. Female pale purple-blue in colour. Hindwing has 2 tails. Underneath pale slaty brown, with hindwing having 2 tornal spots, with the upper spot being orange-crowned. Has curved discal band, white-edged on outer side. Larval food plants: *Acacia pennata, A. torta, Antidesma acidum, Sorbaria sorbifolia, Camelia sinensis.*

♀ UP

♂ UP

INDIGO FLASH • LOCALLY COMMON

Rapala varuna (Horsfield) 28–30 mm

Found across the Himalayas from HP to Arunachal Pradesh up to 1500 m, South India, West Bengal, the Andaman & Nicobar Islands. Flies from February to November in hill forests. Prefers flowers and damp patches. Male shining dark blue, with a narrow dark margin, while female pale steel blue to greenish gloss. Under markings darker than ground colour. Discal band white-edged. Lower edge of cell bar almost touches discal band which is curved and parallel to termen on under-hindwing. Tornal spot in space 2 orange-ringed and crowned. Larval food plants: *Quisqualis indica, Zizyphus rugosa, Z.xylopyrus, Sapindus laurifolia, Lantana camara.*

UN

♂ UP

♀ UP

♂ UP

COMMON FLASH • LOCALLY COMMON

Bidaspa nissa (Kollar) 34–38 mm

UN

Found across the Himalayas from J&K to Arunachal Pradesh, from 500 m to 2400 m. Flies throughout the year. Usually encountered on flowering bushes and shrubs in oak forests. Male bluish-purple with dark border and with an orange discal patch on forewing. Female paler. Underneath slaty or greenish brown with very narrow discal band with white outer border. End-cell bars small. Larval food plant: *Rosa moschata*.

♂ UP

♂ UN

RED HIMALAYAN FLASH • LOCALLY COMMON

Bidaspa micans (Bremer & Grey) 25–34 mm

Occurs in the western Himalayas from J&K to Uttarakhand, between 1200 m and 2600 m. Flies from April to July. Prefers flowering bushes in openings in temperate forests where many individuals may congregate. Upper-forewing brown with orange discal patch with black veins, while the hindwing has a marginal orange band. Underneath pale brown with orangish brown discal line white-edged outwardly, and in middle of forewing, while being continuous in hindwing. End-cell bars prominent. Tornal spot orange-crowned. Larval food plant: (*Rubus* spp?).

UP

UN

LONG-BANDED SILVERLINE • LOCALLY COMMON

***Spindasis lohita* (Horsfield)** 30–42 mm

Found across the Himalayas from Uttarakhand to Arunachal Pradesh up to 1600 m, West Bengal, and peninsular India up to Madhya Pradesh. Flies from March to October. Double-tailed, with large orange lobe and 2 black tornal spots. Underneath creamy white to cinnamon red, having silvery lines edged with black and red. Underneath, hindwing band starts from wing base and touches long central band near tornus. Forewing has blue shot on dark brown wing. Female is dull brown with an orange tornal lobe with black spots. Larval food plants: *Dioscorea* spp., *Xylia* spp., *Psidium guajava*.

♂ UP

♂

COMMON SILVERLINE • COMMON

***Spindasis vulcanus* (Fabricius)** 26–34 mm

Found across India up to 2700 m in the Himalayas, except in arid regions, and Northeast India. Flies from March to October. Prefers degraded forest. Settles on bushes, flowers and wet ground. Hindwing lobed with 2 tails. Underneath is light yellow with rich chestnut bands bordered black, and with central silver lining. Tornal spot orange-crowned. Upperside dark with orange bands. Male has blue on upperside. Female larger in size than male. Larval food plants: *Cadaba fruiticosa, Zizyphus mauritiana, Z. rugosa, Canthium coromandelicum, Allophylus cobbe, Clerodendrum indicum, C. inerme.*

♂ UP

UN

COMMON SHOT SILVERLINE • LOCALLY COMMON

Spindasis ictis (Hewitson) 27–35 mm

Found across India and the Himalayan foothills up to 700 m. Flies from April to October. Prefers degraded and open forests. During dry season, comes down to wet ground along streams. Hindwing double-tailed and with black tornal spot. Underneath is rufous-brown. Band markings edged with black and silver central line. Outer basal band underneath hindwing broken into 3 spots. Upperside of male dusted with purplish-blue scales on forewing, while in female, blue dusting less. Orange patch on apex of forewing and more extensive in female.

♂ UP

♂ UN

UN

SILVER-GREY SILVERLINE • LOCALLY COMMON

Spindasis nipalicus (Moore) 36–42 mm

Found across India from HP to Arunachal Pradesh between 1000 m and 2400 m. Flies from April to October. Prefers forest openings and flowers. Double-tailed butterfly with large orange lobe and 2 black spots. No costal streak present from base to central bar underneath forewing. Outer basal band divided into 3 spots. Underneath are pale sulphur yellow bands in same colour as the ground. Male dark brown with bluish gloss while female pale blue. Orange patch prominent on upper-forewing.

♂ UP

♂

COMMON COPPER • COMMON

Lycaena phlaeas **(Linnaeus)** 26–30 mm

Occurs throughout the Himalayas from J&K to Arunachal Pradesh between 300 m and 4300 m. Flies from March to December. Prefers open, rocky habitat and roadsides, where it settles on flowers. Tailless butterfly of shining copper with black spots and greenish scales in discal area. Female brighter than male. Under-hindwing greyish brown with small black spots, marginal copper band and no white band. Under-forewing has many large black spots. Larval food plant: *Rumex hastatus.*

♀ **UP**

♂ **UP**

♀ **UN**

WHITE-BORDERED COPPER • COMMON

Lycaena pavana **(Kollar)** 37–40 mm

Occurs throughout the Himalayas from J&K to Arunachal Pradesh between 1500 m and 2800 m. Flies from March to October. Keeps to grassy patches and low-level flowering plants. Under-forewing orange with many black spots. Under-hindwing pale fawn grey with many white-bordered black spots, white band between discal row of spots, and submarginal double row of spots. Upper-forewing of the male is reddish-copper with a brown border that has an irregular band of spots. Upper-hindwing brown with a copperish tinge in cell and basal area, and a purplish sheen along margin. In female, upper-hindwing brown, with copper-orange only in discal area and cell.

♂ **UP**

♂ **UN**

ORANGE-BORDERED ARGUS • FAIRLY COMMON

Aricia agestis (Bergstrasser) 25–30 mm

Occurs in the western Himalayas from J&K to Uttarakhand from 700 m to 3000 m. Flies from March to October. Prefers open hillsides where it stays close to ground, nectar-feeding on flowers. Underneath, dark brown with white-ringed black spots and white patch on under-hindwing at base of discal region. Line of orange marginal spots on both wings. These spots not conspicuous in males. Female slightly larger. Larval food plants: *Erodium bryoniifolium, E. cicutarium.*

♀ **UP**

♀ **UN**

PURPLE SAPPHIRE • COMMON

Heliophorus epicles (Godart) 28–34 mm

Occurs throughout the Himalayas from J&K to Arunachal Pradesh. Flies from March to October. Prefers forest openings. Keeps to ground vegetation. Bright yellow underneath, with no discal markings. Prominent red marginal area very dark and continues from underside. Male shining purple with broad, dark, and often with an orange area beyond cell. Red margin prominent on hindwing. Female dark brown with wide orange discal patch on forewing and a broad orange marginal band on upper-hindwing. Larval food plants: *Polygonum* spp., *Rumex hastatus.*

♂

♂ **UN**

GREEN SAPPHIRE • FAIRLY COMMON

Heliophorus androcles (Doubleday & Hewitson) 30–35 mm

♂ UP

♂ UP

Occurs throughout the Himalayas, J&K to Arunachal Pradesh between 1300 m and 3700 m. Flies from March to October. Prefers forest edges and openings. Underneath, bright yellow with dark discal line. Tornal spot on under-forewing prominent. Female on upperside dark brown with broad orange discal patches on both wings. Male brilliant metallic green-blue on upperside with orange red tornal border on the hindwing.

SORREL SAPPHIRE • VERY COMMON

Heliophorus sena (Kollar) 28–33 mm

Occurs in the western Himalayas from J&K to Uttarakhand from 600 m to 2400 m, from March to November. Prefers forest edges, gardens, sunny, dry, rocky roadsides where its larval food plant, *Rumex hastatus* grows. Underneath, greenish ochre with a prominent black-margined white band and broad marginal band of red crescents outlined by black, which is outlined with white line running from costa to dorsum on both wings. Male dark shining violet with black border on upper-hindwing along with black marginal crescents framed in red. Female brownish.

♀ UP

♀ UP

♀ UN

POWDERY GREEN SAPPHIRE • COMMON

***Heliophorus tamu* (Kollar)** 34–40 mm

Occurs throughout the Himalayas from J&K to Arunachal Pradesh, northern West Bengal up to Nagaland. Flies between 1500 m and 2650 m from April to October. Prefers openings, paths, edges, and shrubberies in temperate forests. Comes to wet ground along streams, and visits flowers. More common in inner ranges of the Himalayas. Male dark blackish brown on upperside, with powdery metallic green scales. Female duller and darker than Green Sapphire. Underneath, ochre-yellow with only a faint black bar and black-bordered red crescents. Larval food plant: *Rumex* spp.

♂ **UP**

UN

♀ **UP**

COMMON PIERROT • VERY COMMON

Castalius rosimon (Fabricius) 24–34 mm

UP

UN

Distributed across India up to 2500 m in the Himalayas. Flies from January to December in plains. Flies low, close to ground, visits flowers and bird droppings. Underside white, with conspicuous black markings, some of which are square in shape. Green spot present on tornus on under-hindwing. Wet season forms more heavily marked. Has white tip to black tail on hindwing. Larval food plants: *Zizyphus jujuba, Z. mauritiana* and *Z. rugosa.*

ZEBRA BLUE • COMMON

*Leptotes plinius (*Fabricus) 22–30 mm

Distributed across India up to 2000 m in the Himalayas. Flies throughout the year close to ground in open, dry and rocky areas, forest and road edges. Visits flowers. Underside of wings has zebra-like brown and white markings at right angles to costa. Male has pale violet translucent blue wings on upperside. Female has brownish upperside, with dark, spotted white discal area. Larval food plants: *Albizia lebbeck, Indigofera* spp., *Sesbania bispinosa, Mimosa* spp., *Dyerophytum indicum, Plumbago zeylanica.*

♂ UP

♂

RED PIERROT • LOCALLY COMMON

Talicada nyseus (Guérin-Méneville) 30–36 mm

Distributed across peninsular India, Orissa, West Bengal and Northeast India. Recently recorded from Chandigarh, Haryana, Delhi, UP, foothills and river valleys of Uttarakhand and HP up to 1000 m. Flies throughout the year even in urban gardens, forest nurseries, openings,and degraded deciduous and evergreen forests. Keeps low to ground on flowers. White butterfly with broad orange-red area on lower hindwings and black markings and spots on forewing. Black spots on white area on both wings. Female has more extensive red-orange patch on hindwing than male. Larval food plants: *Kalanchoe laciniata, K. pinnata.*

♀ **UP**

UN

ROUNDED PIERROT • UNCOMMON COMMON

Tarucus nara (Kollar) 22–28 mm

Distributed across India except in arid Northwest. In the Himalayas from HP to Sikkim up to 2100 m. On the wing throughout the year. Flies low close to ground over herbaceous vegetation and grass. Visits flowers in forest edges and openings. Has prominent sharp streaking on underside instead of black spots. Black streak in cell of underside of forewing. Male dull purplish blue with cell spot, while female dull brown on upperside. Larval food plant: *Zizyphus* spp.

♀ **UP**

♀ **UN**

♀ **UN**

COMMON LINEBLUE • COMMON

Prosotas nora (C. felder) 18–25 mm

Distributed across India up to 2500 m in the Himalayas. Flies throughout the year. Usually seen on flowers of small-sized trees, bushes and wet ground. Underneath pale brown with basal and discal bands consisting of two dark thin brown lines within a pair of whitish outer lines. Small black tornal spot prominant along with metallic spots on dorsum. Hindwing tailed. Male deep blue on upperwings, while female similar, with wider dark border on upper-forewing and lacking blue on hindwing. Larval food plants: *Acacia catechu, A. torta, Mimosa* spp., *Pithecolobium dulce.*

♂ UP

♂ UN

UN

TAILLESS LINEBLUE • LOCALLY COMMON

Prosotas dubiosa indica (Evans) 22–26 mm

Distributed across India except in arid regions, and up to 1500 m in the Himalayas. Flies from March to October being more common during rainy season. Very similar to Common Lineblue, but tailless. Basal band on under-forewing below cell, extends to v1. Fringe of hairs along wing borders uniformly dark brown. Upperside of male dull purple-blue with thin black line border, and with tornal black spot on upper-hindwing. Female dark brown with shining pale blue on upper-forewing. Larval food plants: *Acacia* spp. *Mimosa pudica, Leucena* spp.

♂

♂ UN

DARK CERULEAN • FAIRLY COMMON

Jamides bochus (Stoll) 24–34 mm

Distributed all over India, except in arid regions, up to 2000 m in the Himalayas. Flies around bushes along forest edges and shade; visits flowers. Underneath brown with parallel white lines broken into bars. Black tornal spot semi-circled with orange on hindwing. Upperside of male dark iridescent blue, with wide black border on the forewing. Female dull blue. Larval food plants: *Butea monosperma, Crotolaria* spp., *Pongamia pinnata, Xylia* spp.

♀ UP

♂ UP

UN

COMMON CERULEAN • COMMON

Jamides celeno (Cramer) 27–40 mm

Distributed across India except in arid regions up to 1500 m in the Himalayas. Flies from March to December. Flight slow and low, close to ground. Prefers forest undergrowth and flowers. Underneath greyish white (wet season) to brownish (dry season). Number of white marginal and discal lines filled with dark bands in dry season. Upperside of male pale blue with thin black border. Underneath pattern shows through the upper-hindwing. Female duller than male, with broad black borders. Black spots on termen area more pronounced. Larval food plants: *Saraca asoca, Abrus precatorius, Butea monosperma, Pongamia pinnata, Xylia xylocarpa, Trichilia connaroides, Elettaria cardamomum.*

♂

♂ UN

FORGET-ME-NOT • COMMON

Catochrysops strabo (Fabricius) 25–35 mm

Distributed across India up to 1500 m in the Himalayas. Flies from March to November. Prefers open and dry deciduous forests. Visits flowers and wet ground. Wings narrow. Underside greyish, with white-edged, light brown discal bars. Underneath, forewing has a pale costal spot near discal bar. On hindwing, 2 black spots white-ringed near the costa. Two large, light orange-crowned tornal spots on underside of hindwing. Male pale blue above with dark border line and with tornal spot on hindwing above. Female dull blue with brownish border. 2 rows of pale marginal spots and 2 tornal spots visible on upper-hindwing of female. Hindwing is tailed.

♂ UP

UN

PEABLUE • COMMON

Lampides boeticus (Linnaeus) 24–36 mm

Found across India up to 3000 m in the Himalayas. Flies from February to December. Migrates to higher reaches in western Himalayas during spring and back to adjoining plains during winter. Prefers to settle on flowers on bushes in forest openings and edges. Has distinct pale band on outer margins of wings on underside. Numerous dark brown wavy bands on underside. Hindwing tailed, with 2 tornal spots, orange-ringed with a metallic silvery crown. Upperside of male violet-blue, with 2 tornal spots on hindwing. Female brownish, with pale silvery scales.

♂ UP

♂ UN

DARK GRASS BLUE • COMMON

***Zizeeria karsandra* (Moore)** 18–24 mm

Distributed across India up to 2200 m the in the Himalayas. Flies from February to December. Sun-loving butterfly. Flies low, close to ground, on grassy patches, bushes in forest openings and scrub. Underside is greyish brown, with rounded black spots arranged in an arc. Male dark blue above, with dark border along costa and termen, while female dark brown. Larval food plants: *Amaranthus spinosus, Zornia gibbosa, Polygonum plebejum, Tribulus terrestris.*

♂ **UP**

♂

PALE GRASS BLUE • VERY COMMON

***Pseudozizeeria maha* (Kollar)** 26–30 mm

Found all across India up to 2500 m in the Himalayas. Flies from February to November. More common in hills. Prefers open grassy patches where it flies close to ground nectar-feeding on small flowers. Underneath pale to greyish brown with rounded black spots arranged in an arc. Relatively larger than Dark Grass Blue, *Zizeeria karsandra*. Male pale blue above with wide brown border on upper-forewing, and narrow border on upper-hindwing. Female dark brown with blue at wing base near dorsum. Larval food plants: *Oxalis corniculata, Strobilanthes* spp.

UN

GRASS JEWEL • COMMON

Chilades trochylus (Freyer) 15–22 mm

UN

Distributed all over India up to 1000 m. Occurs in open dry, grassy habitats. Flies close to ground. Settles on wet sand. Underside greyish brown, with 2 black spots along costa. Black spots along margin crowned with green and orange. Upperside dark brown, with 3 to 4 orange-crowned spots along termen. Female larger than male. Larval food plants: *Goniogyna hirta, Indigofera* spp., *Pisum sativum, Rhynchosia minima, Vicia* spp., *Heliotropium strigosum, H. bacciferum, Oxalis corniculata.*

LESSER GRASS BLUE • COMMON

Zizina otis (Fabricius)19–26 mm

Found across India up to 2000 m in the Himalayas. Flies all year round. Prefers to settle on flowers close to ground. Underside pale greyish brown with rounded spots. Does not have any costal spot or spot inside cell. Underneath hindwing, curve formed by spots is broken by first 2 spots. Upperside of male dark blue with dark border towards apex. Female dark brown with some blue at wing bases. Larval food plants: *Lathyrus* spp., *Vicia* spp.

♂ UP

♂ UN

BRIGHT BABUL BLUE • COMMON

***Azanus ubaldus* (Stoll)** 20–25 mm

Found throughout India up to 2400 m in the Himalayas, mainly in dry arid regions. Flies from March to December. Visits Acacia flowers on small trees and bushes. Flight strong and continuous. Male violet-blue on upperwing with black border, while female paler with brown border. Underneath 2 black tornal spots, 2 black costal spots and pale brown white-edged band. Larval food plants: *Acacia arabica, A. catechu, A. nilotica, A. senegal.*

♀ UP

♀ UN

TAILED CUPID OR SHORT-TAILED BLUE • UNCOMMON

***Everes argiades* (Pallas)** 20–28 mm

Found in the western Himalayas from J&K to Uttarakhand from 1000 m to 3000 m. Flies from March to November. Seen along streams and grassy patches. Underside greyish-brown, with line of black spots running from forewing to hindwing. Marginal orange band with black spots on under-hindwing. Upperside of male shining blue with dark border, while female dark brown with 2 orange-bordered black tornal spots. Larval food plant: *Lotus corniculatus, Medicago lupulina, Onobrychis* spp., *Trifolium* spp.

CHAPMAN'S CUPID • UNCOMMON

Everes argiades diporides (Chapman) 22–26 mm

♂ UP

♂ UN

Found across the Himalayas from 1400 m to 2800 m. Flies from February to November. Prefers openings in temperate forests. Underside pale grey, with line of small black spots from forewing to hindwing. Underneath, hindwing has black spots crowned with silvery scales and powdered by patch of extensive orange along margin. Male is violet-blue above with dark borders. Female brown with 2 orange-ringed black tornal spots on upper-hindwing. Larval food plant: *Trefoil* spp.

INDIAN CUPID • UNCOMMON

Everes lacturnus (Godart) 22–28 mm

UN

Occurs all over India up to 2000 m in the Himalayas from March to October. Prefers forest edges and openings. Settles on flowers and wet ground. Tailed butterfly. Underside white with line of faint, slightly darker spots; 2 black spots on costa of hindwing and 1 close to dorsum, and 1 dark spot in between this spot and spot on costa. Two orange-crowned black tornal spots on hindwing. Male has dark blue upperside, with dark border on upperwing and 2 tornal spots on hindwing. Female entirely brown with pale blue discal area and black-spotted tornal patch on upper-hindwing. Larval food plants: *Desmodium* spp., *Trifolium* spp.

QUAKER • LOCALLY COMMON

Neopithecops zalmora (Butler) 16–30 mm

Occurs from Uttarakhand to Arunachal Pradesh in the Himalayas up to 500 m, the Eastern and Western Ghats. Flies from April to December. Prefers tropical moist deciduous forests, where it can be seen on wet ground, leaves and flowers of bushes. Small tailless butterfly with rounded wings. Underside white with black markings. Prominent black spot present near costa and another small spot on dorsum on underhindwing, 3 basal spots and outer discal band on hindwing. Upperside of forewing dark brown, with white discal area which is reduced on forewing in wet season form. Larval food plant: *Glycosmis pentaphylla*.

UP

MALAYAN • NOT RARE

Megisba malaya (Horsfield) 19–30 mm

Found in the Himalayas from Uttarakhand to Arunachal Pradesh up to 800 m, West Bengal, Northeast India and the Western Ghats. Flies from March to November. The Himalayan subspecies *(sikkima)* tailed, while sub-species *(thwaitesi)* that occurs in the Western Ghats and West Bengal tailless. Resembles the Quaker but has more pointed forewing and a series of 4 small spots on costa and spot in cell on underside of hindwing. Female has wider wingspan than male. White patches may be absent on upperforewing in wet season form. Larval food plant: *Allophyllus cobbe.*

UN

GRAM BLUE • COMMON

Euchrysops cnejus (Fabricius) 25–33 mm

♀ UP

UN

Distributed all across India up to at least 800 m in the western Himalayas. Flies from April to November. Commonly encountered on flowers around forest edges, open scrub and cultivation. Tailed. Underside light grey, with a line of light brown spots that are white-edged and a bar at end-cell on each wing; 2 black spots on costa and 2 orange-crowned, black tornal spots with metallic silver centres present on hindwing. Male violet blue above with dark thin line as border. Female is brown. Larval food plants: *Butea monosperma, Ougeinia dalbergioides, Paracalyx scariosa, Pisum sativum, Vigna cylindrica, V.trilobata, Acacia* spp.

DUSKY HEDGE BLUE • LOCALLY COMMON

Oreolyce vardhana (Moore) 38–44 mm

Occurs in the western Himalayas from J&K to Uttarakhand from 2000 m to 2800 m. Flies from May to October. Prefers flowers growing in rocky areas and forest edges in hills, Large Hedge Blue, with white underside and prominent large black markings on forewing and minute spots on hindwing. Outer discal spots shifted in spaces 2 and 3 towards margin. Upperside of male pale silvery grey-blue, with wide black border on forewing and small black bar at end-cell. Female has white discal area and broad black border. Larval food plants: *Crotalaria medicaginea, Trifolium repens.*

♂

UN

COMMON HEDGE BLUE

Actolepis puspa **(Horsfield)** 28–35 mm

Found all over India except in arid regions and up to 3000 m in the Himalayas. Prefers tropical moist forests where it can be seen settling on roads, edges and wet ground. Flies from February to December. Tailless. Underside white with black markings. The spot in space 2 oblique, directed towards bar at end-cell on under-forewing. Spot in space 3 vertical. Glassy pale blue on upperside. Female has white patch at the centre of upper-forewing, lacking in male. Male shining blue with variable black margins which are broader in female. Larval food plants: *Paracalyx scariosa, Hiptage benghalensis, Schleichera oleosa, Xylia xylocarpa.*

♂ **UP**

♀ **UP**

UN

LARGE HEDGE BLUE • COMMON

***Celastrina huegelii* (Moore)** 34–40 mm

Found across the Himalayas from J&K to Arunachal Pradesh from 1500 m to 3000 m. Flies from March to November. Seen on bushes, along streams and wet ground. Faint marginal markings on underside. Outer discal band on under-forewing does not enter 1b. Black spots are distinct on under-hindwing. Male dark blue above while female paler with black border and pale blue discal area. Larval food plant: *Prinsepia utilis*.

♂ UP

♂ UN

UN

PLAIN HEDGE BLUE • COMMON

***Celastrina lavendularis* (Moore)** 28–34 mm

UN

Ranges across the Himalayas from Uttarakhand to Arunachal Pradesh up to 1500 m and the Western Ghats. Prefers forest edges. Upperside bluish without any white. Underside grey. No spot at base of v1b. Spots on underside larger and coarser. Male dark blue, with narrow black border, while female lighter, with narrow border.

MARGINED HEDGE BLUE • UNCOMMON

Celatoxia marginata (de Niceville) 30–36 mm

Found in the Himalayas from Uttarakhand to Arunachal Pradesh between 600 m and 3000 m from February to December. Flies in foothills during winter. Marginal lunules present. Underside grey, with spot in space 7 and no spot at base of space 1b. Male shining blue above with broad blackish border. Large discal patches on upperside larger in female, which also has a wide brownish margin.

♂

♂ UN

PLAINS CUPID • LOCALLY COMMON

Chilades pandava (Horsfield) 25–35 mm

Found across India up to 2000 m in the Himalayas. Flies from April to November. Prefers tropical moist deciduous forests, where it visits damp patches and flowers. Discal and marginal row of linked spots. Discal spots on forewing broken and shifted and no spot in cell on underside of forewing. Has 4 spots on hindwing base. Tornal spot in 2 crowned with orange. Dry season form in western India/the Himalayas has white discal band joined to spot at end-cell to form very broad dark band on under-hindwing. Male bright lavender blue above with a dark border and darkened veins, tornal spot in space 2 on upper-hindwing, and an entire row of marginal spots. Larval food plants: *Acacia* spp., *Cycas revoluta, Xylia xylocarpa*, grams, beans.

♂ WSF

DSF

LIME BLUE • COMMON

Chilades lajus (Stoll) 25–30 mm

Found throughout India up to 2000 m in the Himalayas. Flies throughout the year. Prefers openings in forested areas and urban gardens. Flies slowly and settles on flowers and wet ground. Hindwing tailless. Discal spots on hindwing lighter in colouration than the rest, and 2 dots placed at right angles to each other on both wings on underside. Male purplish blue, with thin border, while female darker, with metallic blue wing bases. Larval food plants: *Atalantia racemosa, A. wightii, Citrus aurantifolia, C. grandis, C. limon, C. sinensis, Naringi crenulata.*

♂ UP

♂ UN

ALBOCERULEAN • RARE

Udara albocerulea (Moore) 26–34 mm

Ranges from HP to Arunachal Pradesh and Northeast India between 1200 m and 2400 m. Flies from March to November. Prefers moist shady spots in forest. Flight weak. Wings have marginal lunules. Hindwing disc spot in 4 oblique. Male pale mauve, with large white discal patch and apex broadly dark. Hindwing white, except for basal and tornal area which is mauve. Female dark brown, with white discal patch and blue scaling.

♂

♂ UN

DARK JUDY • COMMON

Abisara fylla (Westwood) 50–60 mm

Found in the Himalayas from Uttarakhand to Arunachal Pradesh between 550 m and 2000 m. Flies from March to November. Comes down to lower valleys in winter. Prefers damp and shady *nullahs*. Upperside of male is dark brown, with creamy band on forewing, while female is light brown with white band. Row of black spots edged on outside with pale dots on hindwing. Hindwing slightly produced in the middle. Larval food plant: *Maesa chisia*.

♀

♂

PLUM JUDY • COMMON

Abisara echerius (Stoll) 40–50 mm

Ranges across India except in arid regions and in the Himalayas up to 1200 m. Flies from February to December. Prefers forested areas with shade and undergrowth. Moves in circular motion while perched on leaf. Feeds on bird droppings and fruits. Maroonish brown butterfly with hindwing prominently toothed at v4. Male more purplish and darker. Obscure white discal and outer discal band on upperside. Wings open and form arc or cup shape rather than stay parallel to each other. Larval food plants: *Embelia robusta, Ardisia* spp.

UN

PUNCHINELLO • COMMON

Zemeros flegyas (Cramer) 35–40 mm

UP

Found in the Himalayas from Uttarakhand to Arunachal Pradesh and Northeast from 150 m and 2300 m. Flies all year round. Prefers undergrowth near forest streams. Sometimes perches with wings opened. Visits flowers and wet ground. Upperside purplish brown, with black spots, each having a white outer edge. Underside similar but paler. Larval food plants: *Maesa chisia*, *M. montana*, *M. indica*.

LESSER PUNCH • LOCALLY COMMON

Dodona dipoea (Hewitson) 35–45 mm

UN

UP

Found in the Himalayas from J&K to Arunachal Pradesh between 1800 m and 3000 m. Flies from April to November. Prefers damp and shady areas in oak forests. Markings are narrow and obscure buff on underside of hindwing. Underneath, forewing costal spot alongside end-cell bar separated and shifted slightly inward. Hindwing has tornal lobe and no tail. Both wings together form triangle shape when held vertically. Larval food plant: Grasses.

TAILED PUNCH • COMMON

Dodona eugenes **(Bates)** 35–45 mm

Found in the Himalayas from J&K to Arunachal Pradesh from 1500 m to 2700 m. Flies from February to October. Congregates in shady *nullahs* along streams in forested habitats during dry season. Hindwing prominently tailed, with lobe at tornus. Underneath silvery white bands, bar from costa across mid-cell, and wide bar before apex. Spots on upperside of male white. Larval food plant: *Arundinaria* spp.

UP/UN

UP

COMMON PUNCH • COMMON

Dodona durga **(Kollar)** 30–40 mm

Found in the Himalayas from J&K to Uttarakhand from 760 m to 2400 m. Flies from March to November. Prefers flowers on bushes in open patches, forest openings, and scrub. Underneath hindwing has 2 small black spots near apex and tornal lobe. Tailless. Larval food plants: *Myrsine semiserrata, Embelia robusta.*

UP

UN

IV NYMPHALIDAE

COMMON BEAK • COMMON

Libythea lepita (Moore) 45–50 mm

Found in the Himalayas from J&K to Arunachal Pradesh from 600 m to 3000 m. Flies from March to October. Prefers to remain around forest streams on wet ground and undergrowth. Chocolate brown butterfly, with orangish yellow markings. Orange-yellow cell streak notched on costal side and narrowly joined to spot beyond end-cell. Termen concave below apex. Larval food plants: *Gossypium herbacium, Grewia optiva, Celtis australis*.

UP

UN

CLUB BEAK • COMMON

Libythea myrrha (Godart) 45–55 mm

UP

Distributed across the Himalayas and foothills from 400 m to 3000 m, and Northeast India. Flies from March to November. Prefers habitat close to streams and wet ground, where it perches on twigs and visits flowers on bushes. Similar to Common Beak, but upper-forewing cell streak long, club-shaped, and apical spots joined. Yellow band on the hindwing. Larval food plants: *Celtis australis, C. tetrandra.*

BLUE TIGER • LOCALLY COMMON

Tirumala limniace **(Cramer)** 90–100 mm

Found all over India up to 2000 m in the Himalayas. Flies throughout the year. Prefers flowers and wet patches on forest edges. Black butterfly with pale blue markings. Cell on hindwing much paler. Larval food plants: *Asclepias curassavica, Calotropis procera, Heterostemma* spp., *Hoya viridiflora, Tylophora indica, Wattakaka volubilis, Ageratum conyzoides, Celosia argentea, Crotolaria retusa, Heliotropium indicum.*

UP

DARK BLUE TIGER • COMMON

Tirumala septentrionis **(Butler)** 75–95 mm

Found across peninsular India up to South Maharastra, Jharkhand, Orissa, and the Himalayas, from HP to Arunachal Pradesh up to 2000 m. Flies throughout the year. Prefers forested tracts where congregations are seen on wet patches and flowering trees (*Moringa* spp.). Black butterfly, with dark blue-coloured markings that are narrower and deeper than in Blue Tiger. Larval food plants: *Vallaris heynei, Cosmostigma racemosa, Wattakaka volubilis, Ageratum conyzoides, Bidens pilosa.*

UP

UN

NYMPHALIDAE

STRIPED TIGER • COMMON

Danaus genutia (Cramer) 70–100 mm

Found across India up to 2500 m in the Himalayas. Flies throughout the year. Prefers all types of habitats. Flies low over bushes and undergrowth. Migrates to higher hills in summer. Tawny butterfly, with prominent blackened veins and with white apical spots on black apex of forewing. Larval food plants: *Asclepias curassavica, Ceropegia* spp., *Cynanchum* spp., *Marsdenia roylei, Tylophora tenuis.*

UP

UN

PLAIN TIGER • COMMON

Danaus chrysippus (Linnaeus) 70–80 mm

UP

Found across India up to 2500 m in the Himalayas. Flies throughout the year. Seen in open habitats, where it flies low close to ground, but prefers shade in forest habitats in dry summer. Migrates to higher hills in summer. Chestnut orange with black borders. Apex black, with white subapical white band of linked spots. Four black discal spots on underside of hindwing. Larval food plants: *Asclepias curassavica, Calotropis* spp., *Caralluma* spp. *Ceropegia* spp., *Cynanchum* spp., *Frerea indica, Tylophora* spp.

GLASSY TIGER • COMMON

Parantica aglea (Stoll) 70–85 mm

Found all over India up to 2000 m in the Himalayas. Flies throughout the year. Prefers open edges along all types of forest habitats, where it flies slowly, close to undergrowth. Visits flowers and wet ground. Has pale bluish transparent markings on dark brown wings. Pale streak on wings, with fine dark lines in middle. Larval food plants: *Calotropis* spp., *Ceropegia* spp., *Cryptolepis buchanani, Tylophora indica, T.tenuis.*

UP

UP

CHESTNUT TIGER • FAIRLY COMMON

Parantica sita (Kollar) 85–110 mm

Found across the Himalayas from J&K to Arunachal Pradesh from terai up to 3000 m. Flies throughout the year. Migrates down to adjoining lower foothills and valleys during winter (up to 140 m). Flies slowly in forest and over canopy. Visits flowers and wet ground close to streams. Transparent bluish markings on dark wing. Hindwing has chestnut border on underside. Male has dark patch in tornal area of under-hindwing.

UP

UN

CHOCOLATE TIGER • COMMON

Parantica melaneus (Cramer) 85–95 mm

UN

Found across the Himalayas from Sikkim to Arunachal Pradesh from foothills up to 2800 m. Flies all year round. Prefers wet ground close to forest streams. Similar to Chestnut Tiger but smaller and markings smaller and narrower, with chocolate brown on upper-hindwing. Hindwing cell not streaked.

COMMON CROW • VERY COMMON

Euploea core (Cramer) 85–95 mm

UP

UN

Found all over India from HP to Arunachal Pradesh up to 2500 m in the Himalayas. Flies all year round. Prefers openings and forest edges, where it visits flowers and wet ground. Dark velvety butterfly with 2 rows of marginal cream-coloured spots, inner row of spots being larger than outer. Larval food plants: *Holarrhena pubescens*, *Ichnocarpus indicus*, *Nerium* spp., *Cryptolepis buchanani*, *Hemidesmus indicus*, *Tylophora indica*, *Ficus* spp., *Streblus asper*, *Ageratum conyzoides* flowers.

STRIPED BLUE CROW • COMMON

Euploea mulciber (Cramer) 90–100 mm

Found across the Himalayas from HP to Arunachal Pradesh from terai up to 2500 m; Northeast and South India. Found throughout the year in lower altitudes. Prefers forested tracts, where large congregations can be seen on flowering trees (*Moringa* spp.) and shrubs. Also comes to wet ground. Male glossy black above, and underside glossy purple with small pale spots. Upper-hindwing unspotted, with plain dark scales in upper half and small yellow patch in the cell. In females, purplish gloss area on upper-forewing is reduced. The pale spots more prominent and white. Upper-hindwing prominently streaked all over with terminal white row of spots. Spots on underside of male variable. Larval food plants: *Ichnocarpus* spp., *Nerium* spp., *Ageratum conyzoides* flowers.

♂ UP

♀

♂ UN

♀ UN

UP

UN

COMMON NAWAB • LOCALLY COMMON

Polyura athamas (Drury) 60–75 mm

Found throughout peninsular India from Uttarakhand to Arunachal Pradesh up to 2000 m in the Himalayas. Flies from March to November. Prefers open wet ground close to forest streams. Perches on rocks and canopy of trees on forest edge to bask. Visits droppings, dung, and wet sand. Flight swift. Has pale greenish yellow, very wide discal band, pale green spot on apex, and 2 sharp tails. Larval food plants: *Caesalpinia bonduc, Delonix regia, Acacia pennata, Adenanthera pavonia, Albizia julibrissin, Albizia lebbeck.*

UP

UN

UN

BLACK RAJAH • NOT COMMON

Charaxes solon (Fabricius) 70–80 mm

UP

UN

Found across India except in dry arid regions, and from HP to Arunachal Pradesh up to 1000 m in the Himalayas. Prefers open areas, forest edges, and agricultural fields during wet season. Comes to overripe fruit, bird droppings, tree sap, rock salts, and pearl millet cobs. Upperside black, with yellow spots in discal area on both wings that are broken into separate spots at apex of forewing. Underneath, silvery grey with black wavy lines, submarginal and marginal yellowish green spots and crescents. Double-tailed. Tail longer in females and sharper in males. Larval food plants: *Bauhinia racemosa, Tamarindus indica.*

COMMON EVENING BROWN

***Melanitis leda* (Linnaeus)** 60–80 mm

Found all over India except arid regions, up to 2000 m in the Himalayas from J&K to Arunachal Pradesh. Flies throughout the year. Prefers all types of forested habitats with grass and undergrowth. Feeds on ripened fruits, tree sap and flowers. Flies low, close to ground, especially during mornings and evenings. Shows seasonal migration from hills to adjoining foothills during early winter in the western Himalayas. Wet season form has two prominent black eyespots surrounded by orange patches at apex of forewing, each with large eye pupil. Forewing prominently angled in female. Underside grey, with prominent dark striations and a series of white-pupilled eyespots, large and small. Dry season form rich brown, with dark spots inwardly edged with yellow. Underside pale grey or brown, never with fine brown streaks. Eyespots reduced and obscure. Larval food plants: Grasses: *Apluda* spp., *Cyrtococcum* spp., *Eleusine* spp., *Oplismenus composites*, *Oryza sativa*, *Panicum* spp., *Sorghum* spp., *Zea mays*.

UP

UN
WSF

UN
DSF

UN

UN
DSF

DARK EVENING BROWN • LOCALLY UNCOMMON

Melanitis phedima **(Cramer)** 60–85 mm

Found in forested tracts in India, ranging from the Western Ghats, Madhya Pradesh, and the Himalayas from J&K to Arunachal Pradesh up to 2100 m in the Himalayas. Flies from April to December. Prefers shady glades in moist forest habitat, preferably bamboo. Flight weak and short. Attracted to refuse and bird droppings. Upperside has prominent grey wing borders, and apical eye-spots lack orange and are much reduced. In wet season form, upperside blackish brown and often unmarked. Underside dark brown, finely striated with pale purplish lines and small eyespots. Hindwing toothed. In dry season form, upperside has ashy grey termen. Forewing termen angled in male, falcate in female. Larval food plants: *Microstegium ciliatum, Setaria palmifolia.*

UP

UN DSF

UN WSF

BAMBOO TREEBROWN • COMMON

Lethe europa (Fabricius) 65–75 mm

Found everywhere in India except in arid regions of the Northwest, up to 800 m in the Himalayas from Uttarakhand to Arunachal Pradesh. Prefers shady forested tracts with bamboo, where it flies low. Comes to refuse and over-ripened fruits. Blackish brown butterfly, with white band and a series of eyespots on underside of both wings. Basal line on underside bluish-tinged. Eyespots black, large, and uneven in form. Underneath, eyespots bordered with silvery purple. Hindwing toothed. Discal band pale yellow in males and more white in females and visible on both sides of wing. Larval food plant: *Bambusa* spp.

♂ UP

♀ UP

UN

UN

COMMON TREEBROWN • COMMON

***Lethe rohira* (Fabricius)** 58–70 mm

♂ UP

♀ UP

UN

Found all over India except in arid regions of the Northwest, up to 3000 m in the Himalayas from J&K to Arunachal Pradesh and the Northeast. Flies from March to November. Prefers forest openings and edges on hilly terrain, where it flies close to ground, feeding on refuse, droppings, tree sap and ripened fruit. Pale brown, with a series of greyish white bands and circular black eyespots underneath. Under-forewing has V-shaped white band in discal area and another in post-discal area. Under-hindwing has elongated and distorted eyespots in spaces 3, 4 and 5, while undistorted apical eyespot has white pupil and is much larger than eyespot in space 2. Hindwing toothed. In females, white band continuous from costa to v2 on upper-forewing. Larval food plants: *Apluda* spp., *Capillipedium* spp., *Imperta cylindrical, Microstegium ciliatum.*

UN

BANDED TREEBROWN • COMMON

***Lethe confusa* (Aurivillius)** 50–60 mm

Found across the Himalayas from J&K to Arunachal Pradesh and the Northeast, from 600 m to 1700 m. Flies from February to November. Prefers undergrowth, rocks along riverbeds, and refuse on ground in deciduous and evergreen forests. Dark brown butterfly with white oblique discal band on both sides of wings. Has two white apical spots on upperside of forewing, and whitish basal line on underside of both wings. Eyespots on under-hindwing in series, with apical spot on hindwing larger than rest. Hindwing slightly toothed. Larval food plants: *Capillipedium* spp., *Microstegium ciliatum, Miscanthus* spp.

UP

UN

COMMON RED FORESTER • LOCALLY COMMON

***Lethe mekara* (Moore)** 65–75 mm

Found in the eastern Himalayas from Sikkim to Arunachal Pradesh and the Northeast from 100 m to 2100 m. Flies from June to December. Prefers dense undergrowth, where it flies low and slowly amongst bushes, feeding on refuse and ripened fruit. Underside golden brown, with tornal eyespot bi-pupilled, basal-line almost straight, outwardly shaded whitish. Hindwing has a series of submarginal eyespots on golden yellow band. On upper-hindwing, male has a series of large submarginal spots. Females have white discal line on upper-forewing angled at v4 and broken into spots below. Hindwing slightly toothed. Larval food plant: Bamboos.

UN

COMMON FORESTER • UNCOMMON

Lethe insane (Kollar) 55–60 mm

UN

Found in the Himalayas from Uttarakhand to Arunachal Pradesh from 1500 m to 2700 m. Flies from March to November. Found along forest edges, openings, and trails in oak forests in the western Himalayas. Feeds on animal dung, refuse, and ripened fruits. Dark brown butterfly with single light coloured white band on under-forewing and 2 dark bars close together in mid-cell. Hindwing toothed. Series of apical spots in which apical spot prominent and identical to eyespot in space 2. Male has dark discal line directed towards tornus, while female has white band across upper-forewing. Larval food plant: *Arundinaria* spp. (bamboo).

STRAIGHT-BANDED TREEBROWN • COMMON

Lethe verma (Kollar) 55–60 mm

Found in the Himalayas from J&K to Arunachal Pradesh from 1200 m to 3000 m from April to November. Flies slowly and close to ground. Perches on tree trunks and prefers damp ground and ripened fruit. Has white band across dark brown forewing. Wings rounded and not chequered. Pale apical spots present on upper-forewing. Underneath, hindwings have sharply defined eyespots along margin with apical being most prominent and larger, while 2 to 3 spots are present on forewing. Male has dark band at base of v6 on upper-hindwing. Larval food plant: Bamboos.

UP

UN

COMMON WOODBROWN • COMMON

Lethe sidonis **(Hewitson)** 45–60 mm

UP

Found in the Himalayas from HP to Arunachal Pradesh, and Northeast India from 1200 m to 3100 m. Flies in the western Himalayas from June to October. Prefers forest edges, openings, and roadsides close to streams and shade. A few individuals may settle on same patch of wet mud. Flies close to ground. Reddish brown, with milky lines across wings on underside. Hindwing toothed. Eyespots prominent and arranged in an even arc formation from spaces 2 to 6. Three eyespots on under-forewing of male and, 4 in female. Wet season form darker than dry season form which is bronzy golden-brown. Larval food plant: *Arundinaria falcata.*

VEINED LABYRINTH • UNCOMMON

Neope pulaha (Moore) 60–70 mm

Found in the Himalayas from HP to Arunachal Pradesh, Northeast India from 1500 m to 3500 m. Flies from April to September. Prefers damp patches near streams, undergrowth, forest edges, rocks and buildings in forest areas. Upper-forewing has a large number of yellow spots and yellow veins. Costal bar oblique underneath forewing. Underneath, hindwing eyespots large, with black centres. Patterns on underside of wing suited for camouflaging with tree bark. Hindwing slightly toothed.

UP

UN

DUSKY LABYRINTH • UNCOMMON

Neope yama (Moore) 75–95 mm

Found in the western Himalayas, where recorded up to 2000 m to Arunachal Pradesh and Northeast India, where recorded up to 1200 m. Flies from April to September. Prefers forest paths, feeding on animal dung, oozing tree sap (oak), and moss. Underneath has variegated brown, grey and white markings. Eyespots present along wing margin. Underside of forewings has three black bands. Upperside plain dark brown with eyespots along hindwing margin. Larval food plant: *Arundinaria falcata.*

UP

UN

COMMON WALL • VERY COMMON

Lasiommata schakra (Kollar) 55–60 mm

UP

UN

Found in the Himalayas from J&K to Uttarakhand from 1800 m to 2700 m. Flies from April to November. Prefers open, dry, sunny, and rocky habitats. Flies close to ground, settling on rocks and low-lying flowers. Brown upperside with marginal orange band. Prominent black spot at apex visible on both sides. Upper-hindwing has 4 small orange spots with black centres, uppermost being without black centre. Underneath, hindwing has 6 to 7 eyespots with each having a white pupil with a double yellow ring. Discal line on under-forewing broken at v4 and evenly curved from costa to v5. Larval food plant: Grasses.

TIGER BROWN • LOCALLY COMMON

Orinoma damaris (Gray) 75–80 mm

Found in the Himalayas from HP to Arunachal Pradesh from 1300 m to 2000 m. Flies from May to November. Prefers dense, shady areas in forest and also openings with undergrowth. Settles on undergrowth on low-lying branches or on damp ground. Creamy white, with broadly dark brown/black veins on both sides. Basal half of cell on forewing orangish yellow with 2 black dots.

UP

UN

COMMON PALMFLY • COMMON

***Elymnias hypermnestra* (Linnaeus)** 60–80 mm

♀ UP

♂

Found across India except in arid regions, and in the Himalayas from Uttarakhand to Arunachal Pradesh up to 1500 m. Flies throughout the year at lower elevations. Prefers forest glades and edges, vegetation around streams and water, especially with palms and canes. Comes to ripened fruit, refuse and urine and settles on leaves in undergrowth. Male has blackish upper-forewing with purplish gloss on apex, while hindwing black, with chestnut border that has diffused marginal blue spots. Female has reddish-brown upperside, with black border and black stripes on upperside of both wings, and white apical band and spots on upper-forewing. Underneath, reddish brown with white streaking. Hindwing toothed. Larval food plants: *Areca catechu, Arenga wightii, Calamus* spp., *Cocos nucifera, Phoenix* spp.

COMMON BUSH BROWN • COMMON

Mycalesis perseus **(Fabricius)** 38–55 mm

Found all over India except in very dry arid regions; and in the Himalayas from HP to Arunachal Pradesh up to 1700 m. Flies throughout the year. Prefers undergrowth of forest habitats, where it is found on overripe fruit, refuse, dung, and tree sap. Dull brown above, with an eyespot on forewing in space 2, which is not ringed. Markings underneath variable with seasons. In wet season, white line runs across both wings from costa (forewing) to tornus (hindwing). Marginal series of eyespots of variable sizes and with white pupils, from along wing margins and above this white line. In dry season form, eyespots reduced to dots and white line is absent. Larval food plants: *Oryza* spp. and other grasses.

UN WSF

UN DSF

UN WSF

GREAT SATYR • COMMON

Aulocera padma **(Kollar)** 70–100 mm

UP

UN

Found in the Himalayas from J&K to Sikkim above 1200 m. Flies from May to October. Prefers forest openings along rocky habitats on hilltops. Dark brown butterfly, with diagonal white band across wing. Band converting into two spots towards termen in apical area. Underneath, white discal band has faded outer edge, while inner edge sharply defined and with fine white striations in postdiscal region. Larval food plants: *Poa* spp., *Bromus* spp.

STRIATED SATYR • COMMON

Aulocera saraswati **(Kollar)** 60–75 mm

UP

UN

Found in the Himalayas from J&K to Sikkim from 1200 m to 2000 m. Flies from July to October. Prefers flowers and open, grassy, sunny meadows. Basks with wings closed and tilted. Underneath, has very broad white discal band inwardly margined by thin brown line on greyish brown background, with fine white striations. Upper-forewing apical spot surrounded by 3 white spots. Upperside has discal band broken into spots and apical spot surrounded by 3 to 4 white spots, with inner spot smaller in males. Upper-hindwing with discal band reaching dorsum.

COMMON SATYR • COMMON

Aulocera swaha (Kollar) 60–70 mm

Found in the Himalayas from J&K to Sikkim from 1800 m to 3300 m. Flies from May to October. Prefers open, sunny and rocky forest areas and forest edges. Discal band creamy to bright yellow, narrowing towards hindwing dorsum. Band splits into 4 white spots surrounding an indistinct black spot in apical area. Larval food plant: *Poa* spp.

UP

RINGED ARGUS • UNCOMMON

Callerebia ananda (Moore) 55–70 mm

Found in the Himalayas from J&K to Arunachal Pradesh and Northeast India from 1500 m to 2400 m. Flies from April to October. Has hopping flight. Prefers open habitats and forest edges, where it visits flowers and damp patches. Velvety brown upperside with rounded wings. Upper-forewing apex with double-pupilled, yellow-ringed eyespot. Hindwing produced into a round lobe in tornal area, with broad discal band on under-hindwing extending into tornal area having 2 small eyespots. Discal area has fine white striations, bordered by obscure submarginal and discal bands. The 2 tornal spots lie inside, passing through marginal band. Larval food plant: Grasses.

UP

UN

UN

HYBRID ARGUS • COMMON

Callerebia hybrida (Butler) 50–60 mm

UP

UN

Found in the Himalayas from HP to Uttarakhand from 900 m to 3900 m. Flies from April to August. Prefers open sunny habitats. Dark brown upperside, rounded wings with strongly arched forewing costa, and apex with prominent double-pupilled, golden-ringed eyespot. Upper-hindwing has single-pupilled small eyespot. Under-hindwing has dark marginal and discal lines running below do not touch 2 tornal eyespots, which are prominent and pupilled.

UN

COMMON ARGUS • COMMON

Callerebia nirmala (Moore) 45–55 mm

Found in the Himalayas from J&K to Uttarakhand from 1200 m to 2700 m from May to September. Has a low hopping flight, visits flowers, dung, refuse in forest openings and edges. Dark velvet brown above, with double-pupilled tawny-ringed eyespot on apex. Underneath, has single-pupilled eyespot in space 2. Marginal band absent, but minute marginal eyespots and white spots present in varying numbers.

UN

UN

PALLID ARGUS • COMMON

***Callerebia scanda* (Kollar)** 50–60 mm

Found in the Himalayas from J&K to Sikkim and West Bengal from 1200 m to 2800 m. Flies from July to September. Prefers forest trails, roadside rocks, and wet ground. Pale brown, with pale outer margins. Shows white striations on under-hindwing, more prominent in wet season form. Underneath, without marginal band, having two tornal eyespots and above them a row of white dots.

UP

LARGE THREE-RING • COMMON

***Ypthima nareda* (Kollar)** 40–50 mm

Found in the Himalayas from J&K to Arunachal Pradesh and Northeast India from 600 m to 2800 m. Flies from March to November. Flies close to ground. Prefers forest edges and roadsides. Visits flowers. Brown butterfly with fine striations and double-pupilled yellow-ringed eyespot on under-forewing. Under-hindwing has 1 large apical and 2 tornal eyespots. Upperside has 1 apical double-pupilled eyespot and 1 tornal eyespot on of hindwing. Larval food plant: Grasses.

UP

UN

COMMON FIVE-RING • COMMON

Ypthima baldus (Fabricius) 32–48 mm

Found all over India except in arid regions, in the Himalayas from HP to Arunachal Pradesh and Northeast India, up to 1800 m, from February to October. Visits flowers and wet ground along forest edges and openings. Settles on leaves of shrub to bask. Underneath, pale brown to whitish, with fine striations. Underneath hindwing has 3 pairs of eyespots in wet season form, which are reduced to dots in dry season. Apical eyespots in pair are of unequal size. One double-pupilled apical eyespot on both sides of forewing. Larval food plant: Grasses.

UP WSF

UN WSF

DSF

WHITE FOUR-RING • LOCALLY COMMON

Ypthima ceylonica (Hewitson) 30–35 mm

Distributed across southern India up to Goa, West Bengal, and Orissa. Flies throughout the year, low and close to ground in clearings and paths inside dense forest habitats. Visits low-lying flowers. Lower half of hindwing white, with 3 eyespots, the last having 2 white pupils. Upper-forewing brown, with large double-pupilled yellow-ringed ocelli. Underside ashy, with fine striations. Dry season form has ocelli on under-hindwing.

UP DSF

HIMALAYAN FIVE-RING • COMMON

Ypthima nikaea (Moore) 45–55 mm

Found in the Himalayas from J&K to Uttarakhand from 1500 m to 2300 m. Flies from April to October. Prefers forest openings, edges, and grassy paths. Comes to flowers and wet patches. Brown butterfly, with fine buff striations underneath. Underneath, forewing has double-pupilled eyespot. On hindwing, 2 apical eyespots joined but separated by yellow rings encircling them. Three eyespots in tornal area, with lowest being double-pupilled. Upper-forewing brown, with double-pupilled eyespot and very small spot just below it. Larval food plant: Grasses.

UN WSF

GARHWAL SIX-RING • LOCALLY COMMON

Ypthima kedarnathensis (Singh) 44–45 mm

Occurs in Garhwal Himalayas: Kedarnath Sanctuary (Chamoli District), Benog Sanctuary and Mussoorie. Flies between 1500 m and 2000 m from May to October. Prefers moist temperate forests with ban oak (*Quercus leucotrichophora*). Flies along forest edge amongst herbaceous vegetation. Superficially resembles the Himalayan Five-Ring, *Ypthima nikaea,* but has additional third eyespot, of variable size, joined to 2 apical eyespots (in space 4, between v4 and v5) on under-hindwing. Three apical eyespots make 135 degree angle, separated from each other by yellow rings encircling them. Other three posterior eyespots on under-hindwing in linear series from anal angle, tornal one being bi-pupilled. Larval food plant: Grasses.

UN

UN

YELLOW COSTER • LOCALLY COMMON

Acraea issoria (Hübner) 45–85 mm

Found in the Himalayas from HP to Arunachal Pradesh and Northeast India, from 700 m to 2400 m. Flies from March to December. Flies low and slowly. Prefers forest openings, edges and scrub, and visits flowers near its host food plant. Emergence takes place in large numbers. Male upperside yellowish brown, with black bar at end-cell, outer black border with spots of ground colour. Female heavily marked with black on forewing, and veins blackened. Larval food plants: *Boehmeria salicifolia, Debregeasia bicolor, Pouzolzia* spp.

♀ UP

♂ UP

UN

TAWNY COSTER • VERY COMMON

Acraea terpsicore (Fabricius) 50–65 mm

UP

UP

Distributed all over India up to 1500 m in the Himalayas. Flies throughout the year. Prefers open country, grassland, scrub, forest edges and gardens. Flies close to ground with slow wing-beats. Comes on to flowers. Upperside red, with wings bordered black. Upper-forewing has thin dark border, while border in hindwing broad with white spots. Wings spotted with black on both wings, with black spot on cell. Larval food plants: *Aporosa lindleyana, Adenia hondala, Modecca palmata, Passiflora* spp.

LARGE SILVERSTRIPE • COMMON

Childrena childreni (Gray) 75–100 mm

Found in the Himalayas from J&K to Arunachal Pradesh from 1200 m to 3000 m. Flies from May to November. Flight swift. Prefers open habitats, roadsides and river valleys. Comes to wet ground and flowers. Orange-yellow, with several black spots on upperside. Upper-hindwing has blue near tornus. Underneath, hindwing has 6 pale silver stripes with black outer edges, silver stripe in discal area straight on greenish ground colour of wings. Larval food plant: *Viola* spp.

UP

UN

QUEEN OF SPAIN FRITILLARY • COMMON

Issoria lathonia (Linnaeus) 50–60 mm

Found in the Himalayas from J&K to Arunachal Pradesh from 1200 m to 5000 m. Flies from February to December. Prefers sunny grassy slopes, forest openings, alpine meadows, and hilltops. Visits flowers. Tawny orange butterfly, with small black spots and dark basal area. Underneath hindwings have large silvery brown-ringed postdiscal spots. Forewing apex produced and termen concave. Larval food plant: *Viola* spp.

UP

UN

LARGE YEOMAN • COMMON

Cirrochroa aoris (Doubleday) 80–90 mm

♂ UP

♀

Found across India from Sikkim to Arunachal Pradesh and Northeast India from terai up to 2000 m. Flies throughout the year at lower altitudes. Prefers undergrowth in forest openings and edges along streams and paths. Tawny butterfly with narrow black outer margin of forewing apex and irregular discal and wavy marginal lines on forewing slightly produced at apex. Discal series on black spots on hindwing. Female darker, with pinkish/purplish discal band on underside. Larval food plant: *Hydnocarpus* spp.

♂ UP

♀ UP

RUSTIC • COMMON

Cupha erymanthis (Drury) 50–60 mm

UP

Found all over India except in arid regions, Northwest India and in the Himalayas from HP to Arunachal Pradesh up to 2000 m. Flies throughout the year. Prefers forest openings, treetops, undergrowth near shady streams in tropical moist deciduous forests. Ochre, with upper-forewing having black apex, creamy yellow central band and reddish brown basal area. Hindwing reddish brown, with marginal lines of crescents and spots. Underneath, yellowish brown with small pale and dark markings. Larval food plants: *Flacourtia indica, F. montana.*

VAGRANT • LOCALLY COMMON

Vagrans sinha (Cramer) 55–65 mm

Found in the Himalayas from Uttarakhand to Arunachal Pradesh, Northeast India, West Bengal, Orissa, Jharkhand, up to 2000 m, from February to December. A swift flier, settling on flowering bushes and wet sand along streams. Prefers openings and edges in moist deciduous forest. Rich tawny-coloured butterfly with outer margin dark and narrow and dusky markings in apical portion. Hindwing toothed and forewing apex produced. Larval food plants: *Flacourtia* spp., *Xylosoma longifolium.*

UP

UP

COMMON LEOPARD • COMMON

Phalanta phalantha (Drury) 50–60 mm

Found across India up to 2000 m in the Himalayas from J&K to Arunachal Pradesh. Flies from February to December. Prefers forest edges, gardens, poplar and willow plantations, flowers and damp patches. Tawny butterfly, with black spots and wavy lines with pinkish violet tinge underneath hindwing. Larval food plants: *Flacourtia* spp., *Xylosoma longifolium, Populus deltoides, Salix* spp.

UP

COMMANDER • COMMON

***Moduza procris* (Cramer)** 60–75 mm

UP

UN

Found all over India except in arid regions, and the Himalayas from Uttarakhand to Arunachal Pradesh up to 900 m. Flies from February to December. Prefers shady *nullahs*, damp patches in moist deciduous to evergreen forests. Upperside tawny, with large white spots forming discal band scattered in upper dark portion. Dark wavy lines on upper border. Larval food plants: *Hedyotis orixense, Mitragyna parviflora, Mussaenda frondosa, Neolamarckia cadamba, Ochreinauclea missionis, Wendlandia.*

COMMODORE • LOCALLY COMMON

***Auzakia danava* (Moore)** 80–85 mm

♂ UP

♀ UP

♀

Found in the Himalayas from Uttarakhand to Arunachal Pradesh from 900 m to 2000 m. Flies from April to November. Prefers openings in oak forest and edges and banks of streams. Upperside has dark brown base, pale brown outer area and dark brown discal band. Tornal area on upper-hindwing with greenish tinge. Female dark green with white outer area, characteristic greenish discal band on upper-forewing darker on upper-hindwing.

♀ UP

COMMON SERGEANT • COMMON

Athyma perius (Linnaeus) 60–70 mm

Found in India across the Himalayas from HP to Arunachal Pradesh up to 2200 m, Northeast and peninsular India. Flies from February to December. Prefers forest edges and openings, and roadsides. Flies fast, close to ground, and visits flowers. Has prominent rows of black spots towards inner edge of white post-discal band on underside of hindwing. Upper-forewing cell streak divided in 4 parts. Larval food plants: *Glochidion lanceolarum, G. velutinum.*

UP

UN

STUDDED SERGEANT • RARE

Athyma asura (Moore) 65–75 mm

Found across the Himalayas from HP to Arunachal Pradesh, and Northeast India from 700 m to 2400 m. Flies during rainy season (March–September). Occurs in damp patches in well-wooded areas. Comes to wet ground and refuse. Upper-forewing cell streak complete and narrow, and separated with a rounded spot. Has prominent black-centred, white-rounded spots forming post-discal band. Larval food plant: *Randia* spp.

UP

UN

HIMALAYAN SERGEANT • COMMON

Athyma opalina (Kollar) 55–70 mm

Found across the Himalayas from J&K to Arunachal Pradesh from 1800 m to 2800 m. Flies from March to November. Prefers hillside *nullahs* in moist temperate oak forests. Has smooth, sailing flight. Upper-forewing cell streak divided into 3 parts and separated from spot beyond. Upper-forewing has spots in space, 1b to 3 directed towards termen. Underneath, has white bands separated by chestnut in between. Egg-laying observed in October at 2000 m (western Himalayas). Larval food plants : *Berberis aristata, B. lycium, B. nepalensis.*

UP

UN

UN

STAFF SERGEANT • FAIRLY COMMON

Athyma selenophora (Kollar) 55–75 mm

UP

UN

Found across the Himalayas from HP to Arunachal Pradesh, Northeast India, the Western Ghats and Jharkhand, from 150 m to 2000 m. Flies throughout the year. Prefers forest openings and edges close to water. Upper-forewing cell streak red and divided into 2 with dusky spot at end. Underneath forewing, triangular spot at end-cell well separated. Male has no orange apical markings on upper-forewing and white discal band blue-tinged. Post-discal band on upper-hindwing obscure. Bands on upper wings darker and narrower than female. Discal spot in 2 wider than rest of spots. Larval food plant: *Haldina cordifolia.*

COLOUR SERGEANT • NOT RARE

Athyma nefte (Cramer) 55–70 mm

Found across the eastern Himalayas from Sikkim to Arunachal Pradesh, from 100 m to 1150 m, Northeast India, South India, Orissa, and Jharkhand. Flies throughout the year. Prefers damp edges in dense evergreen forests. Settles on bushes and flowers. Male on velvety black upperside with white band, orange markings along wing edges and yellowish orange cell streak having a white spot at end. Female dark brown, with broad orange bands and spots. Larval food plant: *Glochidion* spp.

♂ UP

♀ UP

COMMON LASCAR • COMMON

Pantoporia hordonia (Stoll) 45–50 mm

Found in the Himalayas from Uttarakhand to Arunachal Pradesh, Northeast and South India, up to 1200 m. Flies from March to December. Prefers forest openings and roadsides close to ground and undergrowth. Upperside is dark brown, with orange bands. Narrow orange line on black marginal border of upper-forewing. Orange cell streak on upper-forewing cut on upperside near the costa. Underneath, orange-yellow with reddish brown bands and fine brown streaks. Larval food plants: *Acacia concinna, A. pennata, A. megadalane, Albizia* spp.

UP

UN

UP

COMMON SAILOR • COMMON

***Neptis hylas* (Linnaeus)** 50–60 mm

UP

UN

Found throughout India up to 2000 m. Flies from February to December. Prefers clearings in deciduous forest near water. Settles on bushes and flowers. Black butterfly, with white markings. Costal streak in discal band on upper-forewing short, and discal spot in end-cell outwardly sharp. Spots in spaces 2 and 3 not in line with spot in space 5, but join termen below apex. Upper-hindwing discal band does not widen towards costa. Underside chestnut, with white markings sharply edged with black. Larval food plants: *Moullava spicata, Dalbergia* spp., *Pongamia glabra, Xylia dolabriformis, Bombax malabaricum, Thespesia populnea, Zizyphus* spp., *Grewia* spp., *Elaeocarpus* spp.

UP

YERBURY'S SAILOR • LOCALLY COMMON

Neptis yerburyi (Butler) 58–70 mm

UP

UN

Distributed across the Himalayas and the Shivaliks from J&K to Arunachal Pradesh between 800 m to 2000 m. Flies from March to June and September to November. Prefers clearings in wooded ravines and in tropical moist deciduous and moist temperate forests. Upper-forewing has 3 marginal spots shifted in and at right angles to costal margin. White band on upper-hindwings expands to upper margin. Has two parallel white lines on under-hindwing margin. Underneath reddish brown. Upper-hindwing discal band broader filling base of space 3. Two subspecies found, — restricted to the western Himalayas larger and unsullied yellowish as compared to — restricted to the eastern Himalayas. Larval food plant: *Celtis australis.*

Subspecies — *yerburi*

UP

PALE GREEN SAILOR • RARE

***Neptis zaida* (Westwood)** 65–75 mm

Found across the Himalayas from Uttarakhand to Arunachal Pradesh. Prefers moist temperate oak forests and flies close to streams between 1000 m and 2200 m during pre-monsoon season (April–June). Upperside markings wide and light orange-yellow. On upper-forewing, spot in space 1 separated from spot in space 2. Costal spot absent above cell streak on forewing.

UP

UN

UP

KNIGHT • NOT RARE

***Lebadea martha* (Fabricius)** 60–75 mm

Found in the eastern Himalayas from Sikkim to Arunachal Pradesh, Northeast India, and West Bengal, adjoining Bhutan. Flies throughout the year at lower elevations (150 m). Prefers forest edges along streams, where it perches on leaves of bushes and exposed rocks in sunshine. Flight slow. Returns to same perch after brief flight. With wings spread parallel to ground, shape of butterfly resembles a triangle with rounded corners. Upperside tawny brown, with discal white band continuing on both wings. Discal band edged outwardly into series of white crescents on upper-forewing and black crescent-shaped markings on upper-hindwing. Forewing apex rounded and concave below apex. Female has larger wingspan, white area on the forewing apex reduced, as compared to male.

UP

COMMON BARON • COMMON

***Euthalia aconthea* (Cramer)** 55–80 mm

Found across India up to 2400 m in the Himalayas. Found throughout the year at lower altitudes. Prefers gardens, orchards, forest edges, wet ground. Feeds on sap of trees, rotten, and ripened fruits, both which have fallen on ground and those on trees. Flight swift and settles on leaves of trees, often high up. Upperside brown, with olive green sheen. Hindwing outer discal band composed of small black spots. Female lighter in colouration than male and with larger black spots, but lacks white spotting beyond cell on upper-forewing. Larval food plants: *Anacardium occidentale, Mangifera indica, Bryonia* spp., *Streblus asper.*

UN

UP

GAUDY BARON • UNCOMMON

***Euthalia lubentina* (Cramer)** 60–80 mm

Found in India across the Himalayas from HP to Arunachal Pradesh up to 3000 m; South, Central and East India. Flies from April to November. Prefers edge and openings in deciduous and evergreen forests. Attracted to over-ripened and rotting fruit and flowers. Perches on leaves of bushes and wet ground. Dark shining green upperside, with red and black spotting on hindwing. Male has Y-shaped discal band of small faded white spots, while female is larger, having large white spots on upper-forewing and red spotting on hindwing. Larval food plant: *Scurrula parasitica*.

♂ UP

♀ UP

UP

BARONET • LOCALLY COMMON

***Euthalia nais* (Forster)** 60–70 mm

UN

Found mainly in peninsular India up to 900 m in foothills of the Himalayas and the Shivaliks from HP to Sikkim. Flies from February to November. Prefers openings and edges in deciduous forest. Comes on ground to feed on rotting fruit, tree sap, and wet patches. Tawny-orange butterfly, with black termen and black outer discal line that forms small spots on upper-hindwing. Prominent black markings present on the forewing. Larval food plants: *Shorea robusta, Diospyros melanoxylon.*

GRAND DUCHESS • NOT RARE

***Euthalia patala* (Kollar)** 80–105 mm

♀ UP

♂ UP

Found throughout the western Himalayas from Kashmir to Kumaon between 1000 m and 2500 m. Prefers oak forest, with high and closed canopy under moist conditions. Comes down to feed on ground, mainly on refuse, tree gums, ripened fruit, and bird droppings. Prefers to bask on oak leaves. While resting on treetops, wings spread flat. When disturbed, flies away to settle higher up on tree-trunk or branch. Flight period is during rainy season (June–August). Mating observed during July (Shimla). Single brooded. Male and female distinguished by pale yellow discal band on upper-forewing in male, all white in female. Pale spot on upper-hindwing of male more extensive than in female. Male smaller than female. Larval food plant: *Quercus leucotrichophora.*

POPINJAY • OCCASIONAL

Stibochiona nicea (Gray) 60–80 mm

♂ UP

Flies in the western Himalayas from Kullu to Kumaon between 700 m and 2500 m from April to November. Prefers well-wooded areas, forest glades, edges, openings, *nullahs* with plenty of undergrowth and water. Settles on bushtops in damp patches with wings flat. Feeds on animal droppings. On being disturbed, flies away fast and settles on undersurface of leaf, but returns to favourite perch after some time. A few individuals usually inhabit the same area. Courtship and mating takes place in July (1750 m, Garhwal). Row of marginal black spots on upper-hindwing is inwardly blue-bordered in male, but green-bordered in female.

JOKER • COMMON

Byblia ilithyia (Drury) 45–55 mm

Found only in peninsular India up to Madhya Pradesh and Gujarat. Found in dry scrub and grassland throughout the year. Prefers open sunny areas with bushes. Feeds on flowers close to ground. Flight slow and close to ground. Tawny butterfly, with narrow black markings in male and dark brown in female. Underside has white basal and central band. White spots in discal and marginal band. Larval food plants: *Tragia involucrata, T. plukenetii*

UP

GREY COUNT • LOCALLY FAIRLY COMMON

***Tanaecia lepidea* (Butler)** 65–80 mm

UP

Found across India except in arid regions, and in the Himalayas from Uttarakhand to Arunachal Pradesh up to 2000 m. Prefers moist deciduous and evergreen forests. Flies low over undergrowth along forest edges, clearings and roadsides. Found throughout the year at lower elevations. Feeds on ripe fruit, refuse and tree sap. Very dark brown coloured butterfly, with pale grey border, which is broader downwards on upper-hindwing. Forewing apex falcated. Larval food plants: *Melastoma malabaricum, Careya arborea.*

COMMON MAP • FAIRLY COMMON

***Cyrestis thyodamas* (Boisduval)** 50–60 mm

UP

Found all over India except in arid regions, and in the Himalayas from J&K to Arunachal Pradesh, Northeast India up to 2700 m. Occurs throughout the year. Prefers forested areas with water. Flies with jerky flaps and glides. Comes on to wet ground, but also prefers to settle on leaves of trees with wings spread. A semi-transparent white butterfly, with fine black line markings running vertically from apex to tornus through both wings. Outline wavy on wings. Hindwing tailed and lobed. Golden brown markings along outer margin of hindwing. Larval food plant: *Ficus* spp.

TABBY • FAIRLY COMMON

Pseudergolis wedah (Kollar) 55–65 mm

Found across the Himalayas from HP to Arunachal Pradesh and Northeast India from 400 m to 2000 m. Flies from April to December. Prefers rocky and stony surfaces close to streams along forest edges. Flies low and settles on leaves close to ground. Rich golden brown butterfly, with fine black lines and spots. Four fine dark bars in cell of both wings. Larval food plant: *Debregeasia bicolor.*

UP

WESTERN COURTIER • LOCALLY COMMON

Sephisa dichroa (Kollar) 60–75 mm

Found in the western Himalayas from J&K to Uttarakhand. Flies from 1500 m to 2700 m from April to October. Prefers openings and edges in ban oak forests. Flies over canopy and settles on oak treetops. Comes on to ground on wet patches, refuse, ripe fruit and tree sap. Dark butterfly, with extensive tawny markings. Upperside has apical spots that are tawny in male but white in female. Upper-hindwing tawny with blackened veins. Larval food plants: *Quercus leucotrichophora, Celtis australis.*

UP

NYMPHALIDAE

COMMON JESTER • COMMON

***Symbrenthia hippoclus* (Cramer)** 45–55 mm

Found in the Himalayas from HP to Arunachal Pradesh, Northeast India and Eastern Ghats from 150 m to 1500 m. Flies from March to December. Prefers forest *nullahs* and edges. Visits flowers and damp patches. Upperside dark with tawny bands, while underside yellow with dark reddish irregular markings and thick reddish line near base of under-hindwing from apex to under-forewing. Larval food plant: *Debregeasia bicolor.*

UP

UN

INDIAN RED ADMIRAL • COMMON

***Vanessa indica* (Herbst)** 55–65 mm

UP

UN

Occurs in hilly regions of India from J&K to Arunachal Pradesh in the Himalayas up to 3900 m, South and Northeast India. Flies throughout the year up to 2000 m. Prefers forest edges, openings, banks along streams, and meadows. Settles close to ground. Visits flowers and rotten fruit. Dark brown butterfly with black upper-forewing basal area with 3 black spots on reddish discal area. Upper-hindwing border reddish with black spots. Larval food plants: *Urtica dioica, Girardinia diversifolia, Boehmeria* spp.

PAINTED LADY • COMMON

Vanessa cardui (Linnaeus) 55–70 mm

Found all over India from 4500 m in the Himalayas to coastal areas. Flies throughout the year. Prefers forest openings and alpine meadows. Feeds on rotting fruit and flowers. Upperside pale orangish buff, with black spots. Forewing with black apex with 3 white conjoined spots and 4 white sub-marginal spots. Larval food plants: *Artemesia* spp., *Blumea* spp., *Gnaphalium* spp., *Tricholepis* spp., *Zornia gibbosa, Debregeasia bicolor, Girardinia diversifolia.*

UP

INDIAN TORTOISESHELL • COMMON

Aglais cashmiriensis (Kollar) 55–65 mm

Found in the Himalayas from J&K to Sikkim. Occurs from 150 m to 5300 m. Flies throughout the year. Prefers open areas and flies close to ground. Congregates in large numbers on alpine meadows in late spring (May). Brownish butterfly, with orange, black, and yellow markings. Hindwing toothed and forewing produced at v6. Hindwing with submarginal blue-centred black spots inwardly bordered brown. Larval food plant: *Urtica* spp.

UP

UP

LARGE TORTOISESHELL • UNCOMMON

***Nymphalis xanthomelas* (Denis & Schiffermüller)** 60–70 mm

Found in the western Himalayas from J&K to Uttarakhand. Prefers forest openings, alpine meadows, rocky areas from 2000 m to 3600 m. Flies from February to September close to ground and settles on damp patches and rocks. Orangish butterfly, with black spots and markings on upper-forewing, bluish outer margins, with inner black border and large black spot on mid-costa of hindwing. Shape similar to that of Indian Tortoiseshell. Larval food plants: *Pistacia integerrima*, *Salix* spp.

BLUE ADMIRAL • UNCOMMON

***Kaniska canace* (Linnaeus)** 60–75 mm

UP

Found in the Himalayas from J&K to Arunachal Pradesh, Northeast India and hills of southern India up to 3000 m. Flies low, close to ground near water and prefers forest openings and paths. Comes down to ground to feed on rotting fruit and tree sap. Flight period from March to December. Usually seen singly. A blackish blue butterfly, with shining silvery blue discal band across both wings. Series of black spots on discal band, which are more prominent on upper-hindwing. Forewing apex concave along termen. Hindwing with small tail. Underside mottled with dark brown and black, camouflaging with tree-trunks while perched with wings closed. Larval food plants: *Dioscorea deltoidea, Smilax* spp.

BLUE PANSY • COMMON

Junonia orithiya (Linnaeus) 45–60 mm

Found all across India up to 2000 m in the Himalayas. On the wing throughout the year. Prefers dry areas with grass along forest edge and scrub. Flies close to ground and prefers flowers and wet ground. Upper-hindwing brilliant blue and upper-forewing velvet black, while apex pale with white bands. Pair of blue-centred red eyespots on all wings. Female larger, with more prominent eyespots and more extensive black basal area than in male. Larval food plants: *Hygrophila auriculata, Justicia procumbens, J. migrantha, Lepidagathis prostrata, Nelsonia campestris, Sida rhombifolia, Mimosa pudica.*

♂ UP

YELLOW PANSY • COMMON

Junonia hierta (Fabricius) 45–60 mm

Found all over India up to 2000 m in the Himalayas all year round. Prefers dry, stony and grassy rocky areas. Flies close to ground. Upperside yellow, with black forewing apex with yellow markings and border. Distinct oval blue patch on upper-hindwing, which is larger in male. Female duller, with 2 small eyespots in spaces 2 and 5 on upperside of both wings. Larval food plants: *Barleria* spp., *Hygrophila auriculata, Ruellia prostrata.*

♂ UP

♂ UN

♂

CHOCOLATE PANSY • COMMON

***Junonia iphita* (Cramer)** 55–80 mm

UP

Ranges across India except in arid regions, and up to 2000 m in the Himalayas. Prefers deciduous forests. Usually flies close to forest undergrowth, edges and paths. Prefers to feed on flowers and wet ground. Brown butterfly, with paler outer areas. Small spots on inner margin of hindwing. Forewing apex, hindwing tornus slightly produced. When wings closed underside gives leafy appearance.

LEMON PANSY • COMMON

***Junonia lemonias* (Linnaeus)** 40–60 mm

UP

Found across India up to 2000 m in the Himalayas. Flies throughout the year. Prefers forested tracts along edges. Comes to wet ground in dry season. Brown butterfly, with prominent peacock eyespot on each wing. Pale yellow spotting on upper-forewing. Margins of wings on upperside bordered by 3 parallel black lines. Forewing slightly concave, and hindwing slightly produced at tornus. Larval food plants: *Barleria prionitis, Hygrophila auriculata, Justicia neesii, J. procumbens, Lepidagathis cuspidatas, L. prostrata, Nelsonia campestris, Sida rhombifolia, Corchorus capsularis.*

GREY PANSY • LOCALLY COMMON

Junonia atlites (Linnaeus) 55–65 mm

UP

Found across India except in drier regions, up to 1500 m in the Himalayas. Prefers open areas with water, like freshwater marshes, ponds, paddy fields and forest openings. Flies low, close to ground. Occurs throughout the year, but more common during monsoons. Greyish white butterfly, with dark brown markings and lines and row of discal spots, half black in outer- and half orange on innerside, or may even just be reduced to rings with dots in centre on both wings.

PEACOCK PANSY • COMMON

Junonia almana (Linnaeus) 60–65 mm

UP DSF

UN DSF

UP WSF

UN WSF

Found across India up to 2000 m in the Himalayas. Flies throughout the year. Prefers waterside vegetation, scrub, forest edges, and gardens. An orangish butterfly, with prominent peacock eyespot, 2 smaller eyespots on upper-forewing, largest on hindwing. Margins of wings on upperside bordered by 3 parallel black lines. Dry season form has falcated forewing and hindwing tailed at tornus with underside giving appearance of leaf. Wet season form has rounded corners to wings and eyespots on underside. Larval food plants: *Hygrophila auriculata, Barleria* spp., *Osbeckia* spp., *Phyla nodiflora.*

GREAT EGGFLY • COMMON

***Hypolimnas bolina* (Linnaeus)** 70–110 mm

♂ UP

♀ UP

Found all over India except in arid areas, and up to 2000 m in the Himalayas. Flies throughout the year. Prefers forest openings and edges, bushes, roadsides, and gardens. Male black-winged, with white-centred iridescent blue oval patch on each wing. Also has row of white marginal spots and crescents along entire wing margin from apex to tornus. Female larger, lacking oval spots on each wing. Has row of prominent white spots along inner margins of both wings. Forewing has metallic blue markings in end-cell and spotting in discal band of upper-forewing. Larval food plants: *Abutilon* spp., *Hibiscus* spp., *Sida rhombifolia, Portulaca oleracea, Elatostemma cuneatum, Laportae interrupta.*

♀ UP

ORANGE OAKLEAF • UNCOMMON

Kallima inachus **(Boisduval)** 85–110 mm

UP

Found across the Himalayas from J&K to Arunachal Pradesh up to 2000 m, Northeast, Central and Eastern parts of India and the Eastern Ghats. Flight period from April to December. Flies in undergrowth near forest edges and streams. Feeds off fallen, rotting fruit and tree sap. Shows local migration from lower altitudes to adjoining hills during summer. Upperside deep metallic blue to violet blue with orange discal band and black apex. Apex and tornus produced to form tip and base of a leaf when seen from underside which resembles oakleaf leaf when the wings closed. Larval food plant: *Strobilanthus* spp.

UN

V HESPERIIDAE

ORANGE AWLET • COMMON

***Burara jaina* (Moore)** 60–70 mm

♂ UP

♀ UP

UN

Ranges from the Himalayan foothills up to 1200 m (Uttarakhand to Arunachal Pradesh) to hills in Northeast India and the Western Ghats. Prefers moist deciduous forest. Active during dusk and dawn in forest openings and edges, where it feeds on nectar. Settles on undersurface of leaves with wings spread open. Upperside light chocolate brown, with forewing costal margin and hindwing fringed with orange. Underside paler with orange veins. Cell spot and discal areas have white markings. Male has oval dark brand on upper-forewing. Larval food plants: *Combretum extensum, Hiptage benghalensis.*

MUSSOORIE PIED FLAT • LOCALLY COMMON

***Celaenorrhinus pero* (Leech)** 45–52 mm

UP

UP

Found from Uttarakhand to Arunachal Pradesh between 1500 m and 2500 m. Flies from June to September. Prefers forest openings and shady areas with water in moist temperate forest. Settles on flowers and leaves in undergrowth. Dark brown butterfly, with antennae white in male. Hindwing not chequered, but pale yellow. Upper-hindwing has a few small yellow spots. Upper-forewing has 3 spots in discal band with upper 2 being larger than the third. An additional minute spot present just above discal band. 3 minute spots near apex and in line with each other. 2 additional minute spots present below these. Larval food plants: *Strobilanthus* spp., *Daedalacanthus* spp.

COMMON SPOTTED FLAT • COMMON

Celaenorrhinus leucocera (Kollar) 45–55 mm

Found across India except in arid regions. The Himalayan habitat ranges from J&K to Arunachal Pradesh, up to 2400 m. On the wing from April to October. Prefers shady areas near water and rocks in moist deciduous, moist temperate, and evergreen forest. Settles on undersurface of leaves. Comes to wild flowers for nectar-feeding and several individuals might congregate on same plant. Upperside dark brown with many joint semi-transparent spots on post-discal area of forewing. Two series of three, and two very small white spots present on the forewing apex. Hindwing has minute yellow spotting and broken yellow lining along margin. Antennae of male white, while in female only club white. Larval food plants: *Asystasia gangetica, Cavia callosa, Ecbolium ligustrinum, Eranthemum pulchellum, E. roseum, Strobilanthes angustifrons, Thelepaepale ixiocephala.*

UP

INDIAN SKIPPER • COMMON

Spialia galba (Fabricius) 20–26 mm

UP

UP

Found across India except in desert areas. Occurs in the Himalayan foothills up to 1300 m. Flies throughout the year in lower altitudes. Keeps close to ground near small shrubs and herbs (*Bidens pilosa*). Prefers open grassy habitats in vicinity of forest edges and grasslands. Small butterfly, with white-spotted markings on black body. Fringes of wings are chequered. Female larger and darker, with smaller spots than male. Larval food plant: *Hibiscus* spp., *Sida rhombifolia, Waltheria indica.*

SPOTTED SMALL FLAT • LOCALLY FAIRLY COMMON

Sarangesa purendra (Moore) 25–35 mm

UP

UP

Except in arid regions, found across and up to 1500 m in the Himalayas, from HP to Uttarakhand. Flies from April to September. Prefers dry rocky habitat. Flies close to ground with jerky wing beats. Settles on rocks and leaves with wings spread. Dark brown butterfly, with dark mottling on hindwing. Forewing has semitransparent white spots with 1 spot being larger and squarer than rest. 3 spots in apex, 1 in cell, and another above it. Fringes on wings chequered with cream colour. Larval food plants: *Asystasia* spp., *Blepharis* spp.

COMMON SMALL FLAT • LOCALLY COMMON

Sarangesa dasahara (Moore) 25–35 mm

UP

Found across India (up to 2500 m in the Himalayas) except in arid regions. On the wing from February to December. Prefers undergrowth, edges, and clearings in forested areas. Flies close to ground, settling on leaves of bushes and rocks. Comes to flowers and refuse. Dark brown butterfly, with light brown mottling. Forewing has minute spots that are semi-transparent. Female has an additional spot in cell. Larval food plants: *Asystasia* spp., *Blepharis asperrima.*

FULVOUS PIED FLAT • COMMON

***Pseudocoladenia dan* (Fabricius)** 40–46 mm

UP

Found across India except in arid regions. In the Himalayas, found up to 2000 m from HP to Arunachal Pradesh. Prefers undergrowth close to water in forest openings and edges. Settles on bird droppings and wet mud. Has habit of flying in close circles at one place and returning to same perch. Flight period is from March to November. Upperside dark brown mottled with rufous. Upper-forewing has semi-transparent spots, which are yellowish in males and white in females; 3 of these spots present below apex. Another series of 7 spots lies close to discal area, of which 2 spots are conjointed and lowest two are reduced to minute dots. Larval food plant: *Achyranthes aspera.*

TRICOLOURED PIED FLAT • LOCALLY COMMON

Coladenia indrani (Moore) 40–45 mm

UP

Habitat ranges across India (except arid regions), and in the Himalayas between 300 m and 1300 m. Flies from May to October. Prefers shady areas in moist deciduous and evergreen forests. Deep orange butterfly with row of yellow marginal spots and black spotting throughout wings. Semitransparent white spots present on forewing. Larval food plants: *Desmodium* spp., *Xylia dolabriformis, Grewia microcos.*

MARBLED FLAT • RARE

Lobocla liliana (Atkinson) 45–55 mm

UP

form Casyapa

Found in the Himalayas from Kashmir to Arunachal Pradesh between 1400 m and 2200 m. Flies from April to October. Prefers forest paths and edges in moist temperate forest. Settles on eroded and wet mud, spreading wings wide open. Underside dusted with grey scales, giving marbled effect, and carrying indistinct large dark spots. Upper-forewing dark brown with semi-transparent conjoined creamy discal spots forming band. Hindwing unmarked and chequered brown with white fringes. Forewing termen convex. Form *casyapa* in western Himalayas paler and smaller than east Himalayan form *liliana*.

HIMALAYAN YELLOW FLAT • RARE

Celaenorrhinus dhanada (Moore) 35–40 mm

Occurs in the Himalayas from Uttarakhand to Sikkim, and can be seen flying from May to September at heights between 900 m and 2200 m. Prefers shady damp patches in moist temperate forests. Brownish butterfly, with semi-transparent markings on upper-forewing. Hindwing unmarked, chequered with white along fringes, and tornus rounded. Spots in spaces 1, 2 and 3 on upper-forewing. Spot in space 3 separated from spot in space 2 by dark veins. Spot in space 1b hyaline and directed towards dorsum. 3 spots below apex close to costa and in line with each other.

UP

WATER SNOW FLAT • UNCOMMON

Tagiades litigiosa (Möschler) 35–45 mm

Occurs across India except in arid West and Northwest. In the Himalayas, from Uttarakhand to Arunachal Pradesh up to 2000 m. Flies from March to October. Prefers shade in moist patches close to water. Visits flowers and bird excreta. Flies around and often returns to same perch or settles on undersurface of leaf. White patch on hindwing sometimes visible during flight when it circles around one point. Dark brown butterfly, with minute spots on forewing near apex and costa. Lower part of hindwing snow white, with large brown spots on lower margin. Another closely related species, Spotted Snow Flat (*Tagiades menaka*) that occurs in the Himalayan foothills, resembles this species, but has additional black spots in white area of upper-hindwing. Larval food plant: *Dioscorea oppositifolia.*

UP

SPOTTED ANGLE • UNCOMMON

Caprona agama **(Moore)** 30–50 mm

Habitat ranges from peninsular India to the Himalayas, from Uttarakhand to Arunachal Pradesh, up to 900 m. On the wing from March to November. Prefers undergrowth in openings and edges of deciduous forest. Flies close to ground. Occurs in two forms: spotted *(agama)* and golden *(mettasuta).*

UP *Mettasuta*

UP

Form *mettasuta* recorded in March–April. Form *agama* seen in June–July in tropical moist deciduous sal forests in the Shivaliks around Dehradun, Uttarakhand. Form *agama* dark brown, with several pale yellow and transparent spots on upperside. Spotting includes crescent-marking in end-cell, 3 elongated spots near apex, and discal row of spots on upper-forewing. Fringes of wings chequered, with white. Form *mettasuta* tawny brown with less spotting and no white spots on upper-hindwing.

UP

UP

COMMON DARTLET • COMMON

Oriens goloides (Moore) 24–28 mm

UP

Found in the Himalayas from Uttarakhand to Sikkim (up to 1600 m), hills of Northeast India, and in the Western Ghats below Goa. Flies from March to November. Prefers openings and clearings in moist forest habitats with plenty of undergrowth. Settles on leaves and herbaceous flowers. Small brown butterfly, with tawny markings. Orangish-yellow discal band touches cell marking. Hindwing has central discal band. Dry season form is brighter. Larval food plant: *Oplismenus burmani* (grass).

HIMALAYAN DART • LOCALLY COMMON

Potanthus dara (Kollar) 28–32 mm

UP

Found in the western Himalayas from J&K to Uttarakhand between 700 m and 2000 m. Flies from April to November. Prefers low-growing flowers in grassy openings and forest edges. Dark brown skipper, with yellow markings on both wings. Wide streak on forewing covers cell and extends up to costa. Discal spots present from v1 to costa, and between v4, v5 and v6 up to margin on forewing. Upper-hindwing has prominent spot in space 6. Larval food plant: grasses.

HIMALAYAN GRASS DART • LOCALLY COMMON

Taractrocera danna (Moores) 20–24 mm

UP

Distributed across the Himalayas from J&K to Sikkim between 1500 m and 3000 m. On the wing from April to July. Prefers forest edges close to water, agricultural fields, and open forest paths. Flies close to ground and settles on grass. Grey to dark brown skipper with narrow creamy-white markings. White streak on lower edge of cell of upper-forewing. Upperside has small pale discal spots on both wings. Hindwing has discal spots in straight line. Spots normally occur from space 1b to space 8, and those in spaces 4 and 5 are shifted out. Larval food plant: Grasses.

PALE PALM DART • LOCALLY COMMON

Telicota colon (Fabricius) 32–36 mm

Occurs across India up to 1000 m in the Himalayas from HP to Arunachal Pradesh. Flies from April to November. Prefers agricultural fields and undergrowth in open dry areas. Upperside brown with a pale yellowish post-discal band on forewing along costal margin. The forewing discal band linked to edge of wing by yellow markings along veins. Cell entirely yellow. Female paler than male. Male has greyish oblique band on inner edge of central black band on upper-forewing. Larval food plants: *Saccharum officinarum,* bamboos.

UP

DARK PALM DART • COMMON

Telicota ancilla **(Herrich-Schaffer)** 33–36 mm

Found all over India except in arid regions. In the Himalayas, found at heights of up to 2000 m from HP to Arunachal Pradesh. Flies from March to November. Prefers forest clearings and edges, where it settles on undergrowth, flowers, and excreta. This skipper, a swift flier, often returns to the same perch. Upperside is black with a rich dark yellowish-orange post-discal band on forewing along costal margin. Forewing discal band entirely enclosed by dark border, and not linked to wing margin by yellow markings along veins. Cell entirely yellow. Male has greyish-blue oblique band on outer edge of central black band on upper-forewing. Female larger than male. Larval food plants: *Calamus* spp., *Cocos nucifera, Imperata cylindrica, Oryza* spp., *Saccharum,* bamboos.

UP

STRAIGHT SWIFT • COMMON

***Parnara guttata* (Bremer & Grey)** 32–38 mm

Except for South India, found in most states, and up to 2400 m in the Himalayas, from J&K to Arunachal Pradesh. Flies from March to October. Prefers forest edges and openings, where it settles on low-lying shrubs. Often observed basking or feeding on nectar of flowers. Upperside deep purplish brown, while lowerside more chestnut in colour. Hindwing has

4 small white post-discal spots, sharply marked and arranged in straight line. The male has 2 spots on upper-forewing while the female has only one. Antennae short. Larval food plants: *Saccharum officinarum,* grasses.

RICE SWIFT • COMMON

Borbo cinnara (Wallace) 30–36 mm

Found across India up to 1200 m in the Himalayas, from March to October. Prefers open, sunny, cultivated areas with paddy, grasslands, and scrub adjacent to deciduous and evergreen forests. Settles and flies close to ground. Comes to flowers for nectar. Active during sunshine. Upper-forewing greyish brown with white spot in cell. Three spots in row decrease in size from dorsum towards apex. Creamy spot in space 1b on mid-dorsum, and 3 minute spots on apex. Upper-hindwing has 2 white discal spots. Under-hindwing is paler, with ochreous scaling and 3 to 4 spots. Hindwing termen not rounded and extended into stornus. Larval food plant: *Andropogon* spp., *Cymbopogon* spp., *Eragrostis* spp., *Ischaemum* spp., *Oryza sativa*, *Pennisetum* spp., *Setaria* spp.

BEVAN'S SWIFT • COMMON

Pseudoborbo bevani (Moore) 32–36 mm

UP

Found throughout India, including the Andaman & Nicobar Islands, except in arid regions; the Himalayas up to 2100 m, from J&K to Arunachal Pradesh. Flies from March to November. Prefers open sunny areas along forest edge, agriculture, and scrub. Settles on flowers and grass. Upperside golden brown, with broad wings. Spots reduced and minute. Upper-forewing has 3 spots in line from dorsum to apex with spot in space 3 nearer to spot in space 2 than to spot in space 4. 2 cell spots and 3 minute spots below apex. Underside of hindwing has 3 spots from spaces 2 to 6. Larval food plants: *Imperata cylindrica, Paspalum conjugatum, Saccharum* spp.

SMALL-BRANDED SWIFT • COMMON

***Pelopidas mathias* (Fabricius)** 32–38 mm

Found across India and up to 1500 m in the Himalayas from J&K to Arunachal Pradesh. Flies from March to November. Active during dusk and dawn. Prefers forest edges, scrub, plantations, tea gardens, and agricultural land. Settles on wet ground and low-lying flowers and leaves.

Upperside brown with tinge of golden, and greenish wing bases. Forewing pointed with post-discal spots and 2 spots in cell. Underside of hindwing greyish, with minute spots. Larval food plants: *Cymbopogon nardus, Imperata cylindrica, Oryza sativa, Saccharum officinarum.*

GREAT SWIFT • NOT COMMON

***Pelopidas assamensis* (de Niceville)** 42–60 mm

UP

UP

Found in Central, Eastern, and Peninsular India, and in the Himalayas from HP to Arunachal Pradesh up to 1740 m. Flies round the year. Prefers edges and openings in forested tracts close to water. Dark brown upperside, with 2 cell spots adjacent to each other. White semi-transparent spots on upper-forewing. Upperside of hindwing has elongated spot in space 4. Under-hindwing has spots in spaces 2 to 6.

CONJOINED SWIFT • UNCOMMON

Pelopidas conjuncta (Herrich-Schaffer) 45–52 mm

UN

Found in the Himalayas from Uttarakhand to Arunachal Pradesh, up to 1200 m, West Bengal, Northeast India, and the Western Ghats. On the wing from August to October. Prefers edges and clearings in moist deciduous and evergreen forest. Perches on grass in sunshine. Brown skipper with golden shine. Upper-forewing has 2 separate cell spots; 3 yellowish spots below apex in spaces 2 to 4; and spots in apical area from spaces 6 to 8 and 1 in space 1b. Under-hindwing has spots in spaces 2 and 3 with up to 3 spots. Larval food plants: *Andropogon* spp., *Bambusa* spp., *Oryza sativa, Saccharum officinarum, Sorghum* spp, *Zea mays.*

YELLOW SPOT SWIFT • COMMON

Polytremis eltola (Hewitson) 35–45 mm

UP

UN

Common across the Himalayas from J&K to Arunachal Pradesh up to 2700 m, and in the hills of Northeast India. Flight period from March to October. Prefers forested tracts, often close to water, where it settles on leaves of bushes and usually returns to the same perch after brief flight. Basks in sunshine with forewings held upright and hindwings held flat. Upperside olivaceous brown with semi-transparent yellowish spots. Spots between v2 and v3 squarish. Underside more ochreous. Wing margins fringed with hair. In males, spots are more yellowish. Larval food plant: *Saccharum* spp; Grasses.

INDIAN PALM BOB • COMMON

***Suastus gremius* (Fabricius)** 32–45 mm

Found across India and up to 1200 m in the Himalayas. Flies from April to October. Prefers openings in deciduous forests, gardens, shady damp patches, and palm trees. Settles on bird droppings. Flight swift. Underside has a number of black spots on brownish wings. Semi-transparent white spots visible on both sides of forewing. Lowermost spot on the forewing washed with white and nontransparent. Larval food plants: *Calamus* spp., *Caryota urens, Cocos nucifera, Licuala grandis, Phoenix acaulis, P. lourierii.*

UP

UN

TREE FLITTER • LOCALLY COMMON

***Hyarotis adrastus* (Stoll)** 38–48 mm

UP

UN

UN

Occurs in the Himalayas from HP to Arunachal Pradesh up to 1100 m, and in the Western Ghats (south of Goa), West Bengal, and the Northeast hills. Flies from February to October but more common during rainy season. Prefers forested areas and gardens with palm trees. Flies high in tree canopy but comes to flowers in undergrowth and trees. Broken white band across ochreous wings on the underside. Upper-forewing dark with semi-transparent spots. 1 large spot across cell and 2 smaller spots above it. Fringes of wings chequered. Flight rapid. Larval food plants: *Phoenix* spp (palms).

COMMON REDEYE • LOCALLY COMMON

***Matapa aria* (Moore)** 40–55 mm

Found in peninsular India, West Bengal, Northeast hills, and in the Himalayas from Uttarakhand to Arunachal Pradesh up to 1000 m. Also found in the Andamans. Flies from June to November but more common in rainy season. Active during dusk and dawn. Prefers bamboo plantations, nurseries, and forest paths. Settles on flowers for nectar-feeding. Identified by its deep red eyes and plain brown wings that have no markings. Underside more ochreous brown. Larval food plant: *Bambusa arundinacea.*

UP

UN

PALM REDEYE • NOT RARE

***Erionota thrax* (Linnaeus)** 70–76 mm

Found in the Himalayas from Uttarakhand to Arunachal Pradesh up to 900 m, and in the Northeast hills and South India. Crepuscular. Flight swift. Prefers forest edges and openings and palm plantations. Comes to flowers and settles on undersurface of leaf. Upperside brown with no apical spots on forewing, but with large quadrate semi-transparent yellow spots across cell and in spaces 2 and 3; spot in space 2 very large and reaching at least to middle of cell spot. Larval food plant: *Musa sapientum.*

UP

RESTRICTED DEMON • COMMON

Notocrypta curvifascia (C.R. Felder) 38–50 mm

Found in the Western Ghats south of Goa, in the Himalayas from HP to Arunachal Pradesh (up to 1800 m), the Northeast hills and the Andamans. On the wing from April to November. Prefers openings, edges, and *nullahs* in moist deciduous and evergreen forests with thick undergrowth. Active during dusk and dawn. Flies close to undergrowth. Black butterfly with wide, curved, semi-transparent band on forewing that does not touch costa. Minute apical spots present. Larval food plants: *Costus speciosus, Curcuma decipiens, Kaempferia rotunda, Zingiber cassumunar, Z. montanum.*

UP

UP

UN

GRASS DEMON • FAIRLY COMMON

Udaspes folus (Cramer) 40–48 mm

UP

UN

Found all over India except in arid regions. In the Himalayas, found from HP to Arunachal Pradesh and in the Northeast hills up to 1500 m. Flies from February to October. Prefers undergrowth in deciduous and semi-evergreen forests, often close to water. Settles on flowers and wet ground. Black butterfly with white spotting and patches. Big semi-transparent central white patch on hindwing and many white spots on forewing visible on both sides. Larval food plants: *Curcuma aromatica, C. decipiens, C. pseudomontana, Zingiber* spp.

BUSH HOPPER • LOCALLY COMMON

Ochus subvittatus (Moore) 22–25 mm

Ranges across peninsular India, West Bengal, the Northeast hills and the foothills of the Himalayas (where paddy is cultivated) from HP to Arunachal Pradesh up to 800 m. Prefers grasslands and paddy fields near forest edges and openings. Flight slow and close to undergrowth. Often seen basking on paddy plants during monsoon. Flies from July to November in lower western Himalayas. Larval food plants: *Oryzia sativa* and other grasses.

UP

UN

UP

VEINED SCRUB HOPPER • UNCOMMON

Aeromachus stigmatus (Moore) 20–30 mm

Found in the Himalayas from J&K to Arunachal Pradesh between 1500 m and 2000 m. Flies from June to October. Prefers open grassy areas with water. Comes to wet ground. Upperside greyish and mottled finely with brown. Discal row of pale spots. Underside has white veins outlined in outer half, which also has a row of minute dots in disc and margin. Larval food plant: Grasses.

UN

GLOSSARY

Abdomen Part of the butterfly's body behind the thorax.
Adult Refers to the mature stage, i.e., butterfly, capable of reproducing.
Antennae Long, clubbed feelers situated close to the eyes of adult butterflies.
Apex The wing tip or the angle of the wing between the costa and the termen.
Base The part of the wing nearest to the junction with the body.
Bar end-cell Bar or band marking touching the apical end of the cell.
Brand A patch of scented scales (androconia) on the wings of male butterflies (sex patch).
Cilia Hair-like fringes edging the wing.
Conjointed (dots) Joint or connected.
Cell An elongated area, extending from the base of the wing and enclosed by veins. Veins begin from the cell and extend to the costa and termen.
Costa/Costal The upper margin of the wing.
Dentate Teeth-like projections on the wing margin at the ends of veins.
Dimorphism When a species occurs in two forms.
Disc/Discal The middle area of the wing beyond the cell and before the margin.
Dorsum The lower margin of the wing.
DSF Dry season form.
Falcate Sickle-shaped area in the termen of the forewing where the apex is sharply produced and the outer margin is deeply concave below it.
Filiform Thread-like.
Interspace Area between veins.
Larva (plural: larvae) The caterpillar.
Lobe The rounded extension of the hindwing tornus.
Lunule Crescent-shaped markings usually present on the margin of the wings.
Margin The area between the termen and the disc.
Ocellus (plural: ocelli) Eye-like markings (eyespot) on the wings.
Migration Periodic movement of individuals or groups between two geographic regions.

Mimicry Resemblance of one individual to another or to a natural object.

Oriental The part of the region between the Palaearctic and Australian regions.

Polymorphism The coexistence of two or more distinct and discontinuous morphological types in a species, e.g., the Common Mormon, *Papilio polytes*, in which the female occurs in three forms, while the male has only one form.

Probosis A long tube-like mouth part used for sucking liquid food in the adult butterfly. Usually remains coiled in front of the eyes when not in use.

Pupa The dormant stage in a butterfly's development. The adult butterfly emerges from the pupa. Also called the 'chrysalis'.

Pre-costal vein The short vein emerging from v8 near the base of the hindwing.

Scales The covering of the wings, consisting of very small scales of various patterns.

Striated Closely marked with short, fine lines.

Tarsus The part of the leg on which the butterfly walks.

Termen/ terminal The outer edge of the wing.

Thorax The middle part of the body, bearing the wings and legs.

Tooth A brief projection of the wing margin.

Tornus/Tornal The lower corner of the wing at the junction of the termen and dorsum. Also called the 'anal angle'.

Truncate Cut off part of the wing apex.

UNF Under-forewing.

UNH Under-hindwing.

UPF Upper-forewing.

UPH Upper-hindwing.

Veins (v1, v2, etc.) Ribs supporting the wing.

Wing Span A straight distance between the two apices of the forewing of a preserved specimen that has the dorsum of the forewing at right angles to the body. Expressed in millimetres (mm).

WSF Wet season form.

BIBLIOGRAPHY

Anonymous (2006) *The Wildlife (Protection) Act* 1972. Natraj Publishers, Dehradun.

Ackery, P.R. (1984) 'Systematic and Faunistic Studies on Butterflies', pp. 2–91 in Vane Wright, R.I. & P.R. Ackery (eds.) *The Biology of Butterflies*, Symposium of the Royal Entomological Society of London, No.11. Academic Press.

Antaram, C.B. (1924) *Butterflies of India*. Thacker, Spink & CO., Calcutta.

Balmer, O. & A. Erhardt (2000) 'Consequences of Succession in Extensively Grazed Grassland for Central European Butterfly Communities: Rethinking Conservation Practices', *Conservation Biology*, 14(3): 746–757.

Bell, T.R. (1909–1927) 'The common butterflies of plains of India (including those within the hill stations of the Bombay Presidency)', *Journal of the Bombay Natural History Society*, 19(1)–31(4).

Bingham, C.T. (1905–07) *Fauna of British India, Butterflies* Vols. I & II, Taylor and Francis, London.

Blau, W.S. (1980) 'The effect of environmental disturbance on a tropical butterfly population', *Ecology*, 61(5): 1005–1012.

Brown, K.S. (1991) '*The conservation of insects and their habitats*', Conservation of neotropical environmenta: Insects as indicators: 350–403, XIV Symposium of the Royal Entomological Society of London, September 1989. Academic Press, London.

Champion, H.G. & Seth, S.K. (1968) *Forest Types of India*, Government of India Publication, Delhi.

D'Abrera, B. (1982, 1998, 1986) *Butterflies of the Oriental Region*, Parts I, II & III. Hill House, Victoria, Australia.

Dennis, R.H.I. (1993) *Butterflies and Climate Change*. University Press, Manchester.

Ehrlich, P.R. & P.H. Raven (1965) 'Butterflies and Plants: a study in co-evolution', *Evolution*, 18: 586–608.

Erhardt, A. (1985) 'Diurnal Lepidoptera: Sensitive indicators of cultivated and abandoned grasslands', *Journal of Applied Ecology*, 22: 849–861.

Erhardt, A. & J.A. Thomas (1991) 'Lepidoptera as indicators of change in the semi-natural grasslands of lowland and upland Europe', pp. 213–236 in *The Conservation of Insects and their Habitats* (eds. N.M. Collina and J.A. Thomas), XIV Symposium of the Royal Entomological Society of London, September 1989. Academic Press, London.

Evans, W.H. (1932) *The Identification of Indian Butterflies*, 2nd ed., Bombay Natural History Society, Bombay.

Gunathilagaraj, K., T.N.A. Perumal, K. Jayaram & M. Ganesh Kumar (1998) *Some South Indian Butterflies*. Nilgiri Wildlife and Environmental Association, Udhagamandalam.

Haribal, M. (1992) *The Butterflies of Sikkim Himalaya and their Natural History*. Sikkim Nature Conservation Foundation, Sikkim.

Hill, J.K. (1999) 'Butterfly spatial distribution and habitat requirements in a tropical forest: impacts of selective logging', *Journal of Applied Ecology*, 36(4): 754–760.

Kehimkar, I. (2008) *The Book of Indian Butterflies*. Bombay Natural History Society, Oxford University Press, Mumbai.

Kremen, C. (1992) 'Assessing the indicator properties of species assemblages for natural area monitoring', *Ecological Applications*, 2: 203–217.

Kunte, K. (2000) *Butterflies of Peninsular India*. Universities Press, Hyderabad.

Larsen, T.B. (1978) 'Butterfly migrations in Nilgiri Hills of southern India', *Journal of the Bombay Natural History Society*, 74: 546–549.

Mani, M.S. (1986) *Butterflies of the Himalaya*. Oxford & IBH Publishing Co., New Delhi.

Marshal, G.F.L. & L. De Niceville (1882) *Butterflies of India, Burma and Ceylon*, Vol. I. Calcutta Central Press, Calcutta.

Moore, F. (1890–1897) *Lepidoptera indica*, Parts I–VII. Lovell Reeve Co. Ltd, London.
New, T.R. (1971) *Butterfly Conservation*. Oxford University Press.
Owen, D.F. (1971) *Tropical Butterflies*. Clarendon Press, Oxford.
Pollard, E. (1982) 'Monitoring butterfly abundance in relation to the management of a nature reserve', *Biological Conservation*, 24: 317–328.
Sevasopulo, D.G. (1973) 'The food-plants of Indian Rhopalocera', *Journal of Bombay Natural History Society*, 70: 156–183.
Singh, A.P. (2003) 'New Records on the distribution and ecology of Common Gem Butterfly, *Poritia hewitsoni* hewitsoni Moore, from the western Himalayas: A lesser known Taxa', *Journal of the Lepidopterists Society* (America), 57(4): 295–298.
Singh, A.P. & R.S. Bhandari (2003) 'Butterfly diversity in tropical moist deciduous sal (*Shorea robusta*) forests of Dehradun valley: the lower western Himalayas', *Indian Forester*, 129: 1257–1269.
Singh, A.P. (2003) 'Distribution, range extension of bush hopper butterfly, *Ampittia dioscorides* Fabricius (Lepidoptera: Hesperidae) into the lower western Himalayas', *Indian Forester*, 129 (8): 1046–1048.
Singh, A.P. & R. Pandey (2004) 'A model for estimating butterfly species richness of areas across the Indian sub-continent: species proportion of family papilionidae as an indicator', *Journal of Bombay Natural History Society*, 101(1): 79–89.
Singh, A.P. (2005) 'Recent records on the distribution, seasonality and occurrence of Redspot Butterfly, *Zeius chrysomallus* Hübner, from the lower western Himalaya', *Journal of Bombay Natural History Society*, 102 (2): 238–240.
Singh, A.P. (2005). Initial colonization of Red Pierrot butterfly, *Talicada nyseus nyseus Guerin* (Lycaenidae), in the lower western Himalayas: An indicator of the changing environment', *Current Science*, 89 (1): 41–42.
Singh, A.P. & R.S. Bhandari (2006) 'New Additions to the Butterflies of Dehradun valley, the lower western Himalayas,' *Indian Forester*, 132 (6): 767–769.
Singh, A.P. (2006) 'Range extension of Brown Gorgon butterfly, *Meandrusa gyas gyas*. into Kedarnath Musk Deer Reserve, western Himalayas: a lesser known species from North-East India', *Indian Forester*, 132 (12): 187–189.
Singh, A.P. (2007). A new butterfly species of the genus *Ypthima* Hubner (Nymphalidae: Satyrinae) from Garhwal Himalaya, India. *Journal Bombay Natural History Society*. 104 (2): 193–196.
Singh, A.P. (2009) 'Butterflies of Kedarnath Musk Deer Reserve, Garhwal Himalaya, India', *Journal of Threatened Taxa*, 1(1): 37–48.
Smith, C. (1993) *Illustrated Checklist of Nepal's Butterflies*, in T.C. Majupuria (ed.) Rohit Kunar, Gwalior.
Smith, C. (1989) *Butterflies of Nepal (Central Himalaya)*, Craftman Press, Bankok.
Swinhoe, C. (1905–1913) *Lepidoptera indica*, Parts VIII–X. Lovell Reeve Co. Ltd., London.
Talbot, G. (1939; 1947) *The Fauna of British India including Ceylon and Burma:* Butterflies, 2nd edition, Vols I & II. Taylor & Francis, London.
Vane-Wright, R.I. (1978) 'Ecological and behavioural origins of diversity in butterflies', pp. 56–70 in Mound, L.A. and N. Waloff (eds.) *Diversity in Insect Faunas*, Oxford, Blackwell.
Varshney, R.K. (1997) 'Index Rhopalocera indica, Part III. Genera of butterflies from India and neighbouring countries [Lepidoptera: (C)Lycaenidae]', *Oriental Insects*, 31: 83–138.
Williams, C.B. (1938) 'The migration of butterflies in India', *Journal of Bombay Natural History Society*, 40: 439–457.
Wynter-Blyth, M.A. (1957) *Butterflies of the Indian Region*. Bombay Natural History Society, Bombay.

INDEX OF COMMON NAMES

INDEX OF SCIENTIFIC NAMES